LIVING TOGETHER

IN TOMORROW'S

WORLD

LIVING TOGETHER

IN TOMORROW'S

WORLD

A CHALLENGING PREVIEW OF
FUTURE DEVELOPMENTS IN COMMUNITY LIVING,
TRANSPORTATION AND COMMUNICATION

Jane Werner Watson

ILLUSTRATED WITH PHOTOGRAPHS AND DRAWINGS

ABELARD-SCHUMAN
NEW YORK

An original work produced by

Vineyard Books, Inc.
159 East 64th Street
New York, N.Y. 10021

Copyright © 1976 by Jane Werner Watson

Illustrations copyright © 1976 by Vineyard Books, Inc.

Library of Congress Cataloging in Publication Data

Watson, Jane Werner, 1915–
  Living together in tomorrow's world.

  Includes index.
  SUMMARY: An overview of the ways of life that may be possible on planet Earth in ten to fifteen years emphasizing the means of communication and transportation.
  1.   Social history—20th century—Juvenile
literature. 2.   Forecasting—Juvenile literature.
  [1.   Social history—20th century.   2.   Forecasting,]
  I.   Title.
  HN17.5.W388   309.1'048   75-39507
  ISBN 00-200-00162-0

Manufactured in the United States of America   10 9 8 7 6 5 4 3 2 1

CONTENTS

1 COMMUNITY LIVING:

A Sense of Belonging

Community living dates back to the time when mankind first learned to plant crops and domesticate animals. These practices made it possible and in many instances essential for people to settle in permanent homes. Herdsmen and shepherds must move about so that their herds and flocks can have fresh pasture. But farmers must be settled in order to plant, cultivate and harvest crops.

As crops increased in size and became more reliable, larger groups of people could be fed. Not everyone had to work at raising food; some people began to develop other crafts and skills. From those early beginnings humankind has been building civilizations. A civilization is basically the sum of all that a group of people has learned about living together and mutually enhancing the quality of their lives.

A civilization includes social customs and religion; rules, laws and government; and all the arts, crafts, sciences and systems of education. For thousands of years it seemed to be a general rule that the larger the community the higher its level of civilization.

The roots of the words "civilization," "city" and "civility" (or "courtesy") all come from the same Latin word *civitas*. Civilized living—living graciously and pleasantly with others, enjoying beauty in many forms and having a rich variety of experiences in the shelter of secure surroundings—was associated with dwelling in a sizable town or city.

As civilizations developed, most people continued to live outside towns and cities. These rural groups were often held together by ties of kinship and mutual helpfulness. A community does not need to be large or closely built to be a pleasant place to live. Any group of people, no matter how widely scattered, who share some common interest comprise a community. The vital element is sharing.

About 200 years ago the Scientific and Industrial Revolution began. Before that time crafts such as weaving cloth and making pottery were carried on in home workshops. Boys and girls grew up learning the skill of a trade as apprentices. In the late 1700s machines began to take the place of hand labor. Many of the machines were so large that they had to be housed in special buildings called factories. Apprentices and skilled craftsmen were replaced by people with limited skills who tended the machines that did most of the work. Some of these factories employed hundreds of laborers. Workers who had lived scattered through the countryside came crowding into the areas around the factories.

Changes in farming methods as well as the growth of factories combined to cause more families to move to the cities. Young people in increasing numbers left their rural homes and traveled to cities to make their fortunes. Some of the newcomers were interested mainly in earning more money. Some hoped for better educations for their children. Others wanted more interesting jobs or more excitement. For cities generally offered more opportunities to develop and use different abilities and talents.

Whatever the reason, people migrated to cities all around the world, particularly during the past century. During the 1960s worldwide urban population increased by 40 percent. By the early 1970s more than 80 percent of the people of Australia, Japan and Western Europe lived in large cities. About 70 percent of the people of the United States lived in urban areas that occupied only two percent of the two billion acres of land in the country.

Gradually people began to realize that the centers of most of the large cities of the world were so crowded, noisy and dirty that urban living was, for many people, far from gracious and "civilized." In fact, with pollution of many sorts, living in large cities was not healthy.

Perhaps worse than this, many city dwellers had lost the sense of belonging to a warm community. For a time many newcomers to big cities managed to cling to relatives or friends from "back home." As they moved out of these nuclear groups they were often lost in an unfriendly crowd.

In many large cities people lost a feeling of neighborliness and sense of sharing. They developed instead a sense of aloofness and even of mutual distrust. Loss of respect for the rights, property and welfare of others led to resentment and often to crime and violence.

It is unfair to blame all the ills of city living on industrialization. In ancient and medieval times, long before the Industrial Revolution, the homes of working people in the great cities of the world were small, dark, uncomfortable and unsanitary. Even the streets in front of the finest city homes were hazardous to walk along because buckets of wastes might be thrown out of a window into the street at any time. Epidemics and plagues swept the cities and few people lived to be old. Still, in those long-ago times city dwellers did have a sense of kinship with those around them. And most of them did not really expect much of life.

One basic change in today's world is that many more children live to grow up because of improved health care and ample food. And many more adults live to be old, so the population of the world has greatly increased. Another related change is that the Scientific and Industrial Revolution has been followed by the Revolution of Rising Expectations. People of today expect much more of life— not only longevity but comfort, security, education, entertainment and opportunities. They still yearn for old-time friendly neighborliness, though.

Since World War II, increasing numbers of people have been re-evaluating their ways of living. What people value and hope for in life are still the same basics for which they used to flock to the cities. They want adequate food and housing, good employment opportunities, health care and educational facilities. They also want chances for recreation and culture and places to shop. Now, most of these needs can be met far beyond city limits, thanks to advances in transportation and communication. So the push toward the cities has slowed.

In the People's Republic of China, where the government manages everyone's lives, the direction of migration has been reversed. Providing food for more than 800 million people occupies 80 percent of the workers. Every year millions of young people are sent for at

Many city-born Chinese must learn to live in simple rural communities.

least two years to work on a rural commune. Even older teachers, doctors and other trained leaders are assigned to live in small communities far from their original homes.

In the United States, where people have been accustomed to moving about as they choose, the proportion of the population living in large cities did not grow between 1950 and 1975. Small cities, towns, villages and farms now offer alternate life styles that are attracting increasing numbers of people.

Plans for new communities of many sorts are on drawing boards, in the pages of reports and proposals or actually under construction today. The aim is to provide a share in all the good things of life for everyone. Best of all, planners hope to rekindle warm, personal feelings of community.

PEOPLE ON THE LAND

If an eighteenth-century North American were somehow to return for a visit, almost nothing would be recognizable. Two hundred years ago the continent of North America was sparsely populated. Except for the East Coast and some distance inland, the land was nearly empty. Only Indians and a few European settlers roamed as hunters or lived as farmers and fishermen in small woodland villages. Farmlands in Europe and the cultivated sections of Asia were already in short supply. But as people explored the vast inland reaches of the North American continent, it seemed that there was enough land for everyone—forever.

The young republic of the United States held most of the territory west of the Alleghenies as public land. Gradually these territories were opened to settlers, and some large plots were set aside as grants for schools and colleges. Acreage was awarded to soldiers in return for military service. And great tracts were given away to encourage the building of roads, canals and, later, railways.

Under the Homestead Act of 1863, settlers could claim sections of 160 acres of land in return for establishing a homestead. Part of the land usually had to be cleared for crops, and other improvements had to be made. More than a million families received homestead deeds totaling nearly 250 million acres as homesteading of land continued well into the twentieth century. Alaska and the Canadian northlands offered the last rugged opportunities for pioneering in North America.

The Homestead Act gave vast amounts of public land for nominal fees to anyone who settled on property for five years. It was a major factor in the rapid settlement of the West.

By the last quarter of the twentieth century many people realized that too much land that had once been wide-open frontier had been not only developed but ravaged. Wilderness areas once rich in timber or underground mineral wealth have been destroyed by motor-driven wheels, chewed by bulldozers and polluted by poisonous wastes and smoke from plants and factories.

In addition, cities sprawl in all directions. Much of the urban sprawl happened without adequate long-term planning and regulation. Good farm land that once provided food for many people has been covered with housing tracts or shopping centers. In recent years about 1½ million acres of crop land a year have been turned into building sites. This is particularly frightening since changes in the climate of central Africa and sections of India have made large stretches of crop land unproductive. The earth is running short of food for its growing population.

The Drift to Cities

When farmlands no longer produce food, country people move to cities to look for work. Urban life has attracted people from farms as long as there have been cities. In many countries, when a father died his eldest son inherited the property. This custom of primogeniture kept the land from being split into parcels so small that no one of them could support a family. The younger sons then moved into town. The towns and cities were thus supplied with able new workers for many trades and professions.

In recent years many family farms have been bought up by agrobusinesses. Corporations or individuals consolidate large farm holdings to be run as food factories, with machinery substituting for workers wherever possible. Any large automated factory needs fewer workers per unit of output than many small workshops would employ. In the same way, industrialized agriculture needs fewer workers than do family farms. The unemployed farm workers tend to drift into cities. Urban centers unfortunately do not have many jobs that the farm people are trained to do.

Some critics point out that agrobusiness is wasteful. Great quantities of irreplaceable fossil fuels are used to power the machines. By contrast, farms of the People's Republic of China use human energy instead of machines. This keeps the people employed, and the only fuel needed to "stoke the furnaces" of the workers is food.

The Green Revolution and Population Growth

Farmers in much of Asia have a hard time feeding the rapidly growing population. In the 1960s the "green revolution" was hailed as a solution to threatening worldwide hunger. This "revolution" was based on the development of special new hybrid varieties of

Some of the promise of the green revolution has been fulfilled by increasing food production, but world hunger remains a serious problem.

rice, wheat, millet and other grains. To be successful, farmers had to use the right seed, fertilizers and equipment that most of them could not afford to buy.

A few prosperous farmers did use the new seeds and methods. They increased their output dramatically and they grew more prosperous. Many small farmers could not compete. They had to sell their plots to the larger landholders. Some went to work as hired laborers on the large farms. Others wandered to the cities in hope that life would be better there.

The green revolution did increase food production. But population was increasing at the same time. The number of mouths to feed increased faster than the amount of food that was grown. This remains one of the most serious problems facing the world today.

Sites and Services for Shantytowns

The population is growing. More people are moving to the cities. Housing is in short supply. As a result, many of the cities of India, Latin America and Africa are ringed with shantytowns filled with landless and often jobless country folk.

Homes in these shantytowns are huts made of flattened tin cans, cardboard cartons, sticks, straw, mud and occasional strips of galvanized iron. There is little running water, and modern sanitation is entirely lacking. People in these shantytowns usually do not have enough to eat. They have a hard time keeping clean. They have little protection from rain, cold or summer heat. Sickness is common.

Some planners, horrified by conditions in the shantytowns, think they should be torn down. Just where the residents should go is not indicated. Other people favor making improvements rather than moving the inhabitants out. Good roads, sewer systems, running water and small sturdy houses would go a long way to improve the health of the people living in these communities.

Proposals like this for shantytowns are called "sites and services" plans. Their aim is to help people to adjust gradually to city life. Peoples would be provided with decent places to live and encouraged to use their skills to better their lives and their community. Families move into roughly finished small house shells and finish and decorate them. This gives them pride in home ownership. Government funds finance these projects.

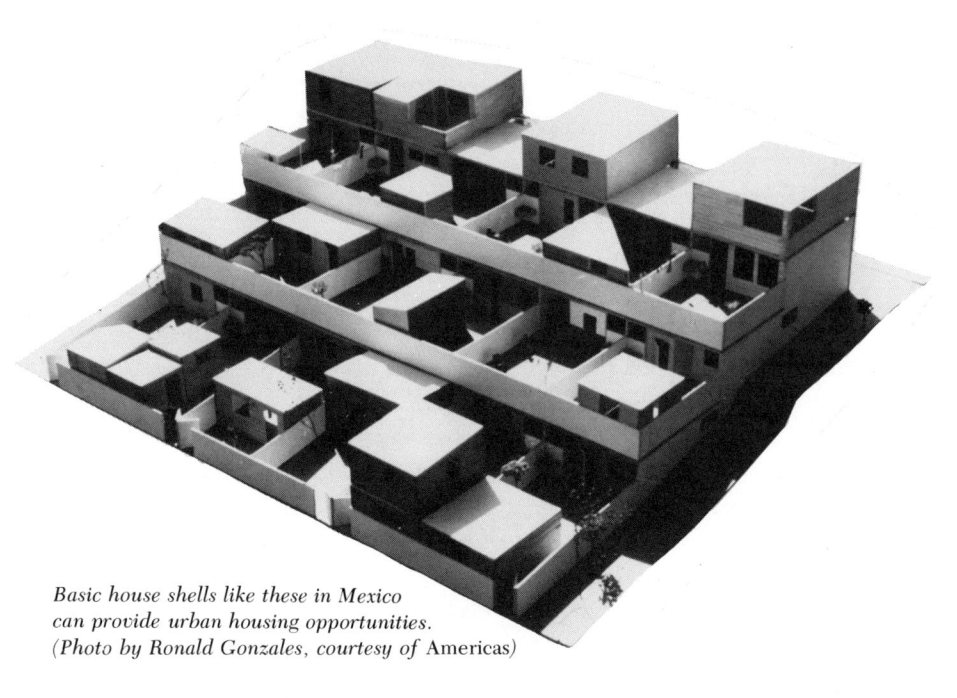

Basic house shells like these in Mexico
can provide urban housing opportunities.
(Photo by Ronald Gonzales, courtesy of Americas)

Some experts, though they recognize the need for this kind of help, feel that it comes too late. They feel that plans should be made to keep families busy and content in the country. They point out that most people are happier surrounded by grass and trees than by pavement and walls. They believe it is time to change the direction of migration back to the country.

Recreation or Ruin?

"Back to the land" movements can cause problems of their own. Many city families in the United States, Canada and western Europe want country places where they can relax. This longing to spend some time among woods and lakes, on wide deserts or among towering mountains has led to problems about the proper use of these lands and who should determine how the land is to be used.

Good farmlands and lovely scenic places have been taken over for holiday cottages or country homes without much thought. To make these new homes easy to reach, highways and service roads have been laid over the landscape in a vast web. Highways absorb hundreds of thousands of acres of prime farmland. Once these highways exist, more people drive to reach recreation areas. In too many cases the crowds destroy what they had come to enjoy.

15

The shores of many inland lakes once provided pleasant wooded sites for holidays. There was good swimming, fishing and a chance to relax. Today many of those shorelines are so crowded with small cottages and campsites that they have become noisy rural slums. The lakes are so polluted that the water is no longer safe for swimming, and fish and other wildlife are in danger.

Coastlines are also in jeopardy. Of the long coastlines of the United States, only 2 percent have been kept for the public. All the rest is privately owned. Hundreds of square miles of swamps and sloughs along the coasts have been dredged and filled for homesites or commercial use. Water birds and migratory flocks have lost their nesting sites or temporary stopping places. Some species are in danger of extinction. And many of the homes built along the coasts are often flooded or battered by tides and storms.

Dry desert areas have been equally misused. Plots of sand and gravel have been sold to people who dreamed of wide-open spaces and clear desert air. Some people have built small homes on their plots only to find that the difficulty of getting water and the drifting sands made their dream houses unlivable. When these homes are abandoned, they do not just disappear. The desert and mountains are scarred in many places with the roads and the clutter of ruins left behind.

Everybody's Back Yard

People should not be kept away from open lands. Holidays in the countryside are good for everyone. But environmentalists feel that the lands of earth must be used with care. We who are living today do not have the right to spoil the earth for those who will come after us.

A start has been made at saving pieces of land that are especially beautiful. Some of these have been made into public parks that are meant to be "everybody's back yard."

Even national parks are not entirely secure, though. Some sections of national forests are leased to lumbering interests for cutting. Other public lands are leased to mining interests. Cutover forest land must be skillfully managed to remain beautiful. The slag heaps and craters of mines are ugly, and developers have not often bothered to cover over the scars and replant the area.

Many recreational areas are seriously damaged by overcrowding during the summers. To save parks from overuse, conservation groups recommend that the construction of roads be halted and that private automobiles no longer be permitted in parks.

In some parks free bus service is already available. With large parking lots outside the park gates, these buses replace all private vehicles within the park.

Automobiles, trailers and camper trucks are not the only problem. Motorcycles, trail bikes and dune buggies chew up ground cover and the root systems of fragile plants. They destroy fields of beautiful wild flowers. They disturb the homes and food supplies of countless small creatures. The noise of these machines is a form of pollution too.

Controlling the use of public lands is clearly needed. It is increasingly recognized that the use of private lands must also be managed. It is not good enough for people to say, "That is my land. I can do as I please with it." Each plot is a part of a larger community, and lasting damage must be prevented.

Free bus service replaces private cars in Yosemite Park.

Environmental Impact

Does a community want to expand its airport or build a new one? Does the city need a new waste-disposal and treatment system? Is a new express highway planned to cut through an area? Do developers have blueprints for new housing tracts on hillside plots? Is an industrial park planned to cover productive farmland? Are homesites to be sold on a shoreline or in mountains or on a desert?

If so, chances are that the planners will have to submit a report showing how their proposed development will affect the environment of the whole region.

There have been zoning restrictions to set limits on the land use in cities for some years. No one can build a store on a lot zoned for residential use. Special zones are set aside for one- or two-family houses and for apartment houses of various sizes. No more than a certain number of dwelling units can be built on an acre. The maximum height of buildings is often set. Zones for business, light industry and for other types of buildings are indicated on city plans.

These zoning regulations are not designed just to keep neighborhoods pleasant. They also are related to the water supply, the sewage system and the streets and highways of the city or town.

State, regional and the federal governments are increasingly concerned with these matters. They are making inventories of their land and natural resources to regulate usage to avoid serious abuse. Good farmland should not be casually broken up into building lots. Buildings or roads should not be built on lands where there is considerable danger of earthquake damage, floods or mud slides.

To prevent erosion farmers have for years been planting wind breaks between fields, keeping fallow areas planted with ground cover, preventing flocks and herds from devouring plant roots and plowing in lines that follow the contours of the land to help prevent land from washing away.

The mutual acceptance of rules for living together has always been an important element in civilization. Today, with world population increasing rapidly, more and more rules are needed regarding land use as well as many other topics. Some people resent these rules because they limit individual liberty. But unless we all abide by the rules for living together, the world will no longer be pleasant or even livable for future generations.

THE BEST PLACE TO LIVE

"What size community would you like best to live in?" This was the question a group of U.S. public opinion pollsters asked a few years ago.

Most of those interviewed did not want to live in big cities. Almost a third longed for small-city or small-town life. Another 32 percent wanted to live in suburbs and 23 percent on farms. Only about 13 percent really preferred big-city life to any other.

Most people judged cities of 10,000 to 50,000 to be the best places to raise children and to have happy, tension-free lives. For the best combination of jobs, recreation and education, half the people interviewed felt that cities of 50,000 to 150,000 were ideal.

Seven out of every ten people interviewed said they were fairly well satisfied where they were. They might like to be in a smaller city for the sake of their children or because they dreamed of a quiet life. But most of the people who lived in cities of more than half a million felt they would miss the stimulation, the contacts, the entertainment possibilities of a big city. Most of those who voted for small-town or rural life specified that they wanted to be within a short drive of a city.

It is important to know what size community people prefer because of the pace at which the population of the world is growing. Within the decade of the 1960s the population of the United States alone grew by 24 million, and it was not the fastest growth rate in the world. Though the birth rate slowed in the early 1970s, the population was still growing because of increased longevity and better medical care.

Great Britain has had experience with new city building for some years. The idea of planned "garden cities" originated in Britain before 1900. Growth was slow until the close of World War II. But the war destroyed homes by the tens of thousands and stopped the building of new homes for more than six years. At war's end there was a tremendous need for new housing. There was also a great deal of unemployment in areas where war industries had been centered.

The government located new garden towns in areas of heavy unemployment and instructed key industries to build plants in these towns. One of the regions hardest hit by unemployment was Glasgow and its environs. A half dozen new garden towns were created in the countryside there, each designed to house between 10,000 and 25,000 people. New Kilbride and Cumbernauld were two of these that soon had new factories humming as well as families of workers filling the homes. Some of the families found it difficult to be separated from their relatives back in the city; they missed the small neighborhood markets and pubs. But government sponsorship made these garden towns prosper.

Since World War II, particularly in the 1960s, a number of new cities have been planned in detail in the United States. Construction has started in many areas scattered from Virginia to Illinois and Minnesota and on to Texas and California. Some of these were assisted by grants from the U.S. Department of Housing and Urban Development. But most of the financial planning and management was private. Building costs rose sharply in the 1960s and 1970s. Government support was uncertain. Soon the financial condition of many of these projects was imperiled.

In the midst of the excitement about totally new cities, many families quietly moved out of cities and back to existing small towns. At least one group of planners felt that if this reverse migration trickle could be speeded to a stream it might be the solution to the problem of providing livable housing for large numbers of families without building all-new communities.

This group maintained that 3,000 existing towns and cities with between 5,000 and 100,000 people could accommodate all the population growth anticipated in the U S. for thirty to forty years.

Small-Town Life

A study of the ways in which rural communities could be modernized to attract more city dwellers has been sponsored by the United States government.

As a living laboratory the organizer of this study, an expert in modern communications techniques, chose a rural county in New England. This county was underpopulated and was low on essential services. The challenge was to make it an attractive place for young families to live once again.

No matter how much people dream of the joys of semirural life, the heads of families hesitate about moving from the city unless they are assured of suitable jobs, good schools and health services. They are also concerned about the variety of sports, entertainment and cultural activities that will be available. They may be afraid of missing plays, good music, professional sports, art galleries, a wide variety of shops and other features of city life.

Many small-town dwellers feel that they are better off than people in cities regarding leisure activities. They take a more active part in community affairs. They can be doers in a small town, whereas in a big city they would be onlookers. They take part in town government, musical groups, little theaters and service clubs. They participate in sports instead of paying to watch professional athletes.

Many small towns have well-equipped schools in which students get more personal attention than in many big-city systems. This left employment and health care as the major topics to be studied.

At Work in the Country

Supporting the family is the major concern of most parents. So providing a wider range of work opportunities was a primary goal of the rural society study. The group looked for businesses that could readily set up small branch operations in a rural setting.

A business is not likely to move a branch to the country just so its employees can garden, fish and ride horseback with their children. The move must be practical and efficient for the company as well. The planning group assembled information to show businesses the advantages of rural locations.

Instead of having all the employees spend hours each day traveling to a central-city office and home again, the planners proposed that small groups of people work close to their homes. They analyzed the ways in which companies could substitute increased communication to replace transportation to and from the offices. They could keep in touch with other offices of the company with conference telephone hook-ups, teletypewriters and computers. (These are discussed in more detail in later chapters.)

No new inventions are needed to make all this practical. All the equipment and technology exist. Some new business practices will be needed to popularize the idea of small rural branches.

Health Care at the Door

Good doctors and a near-by hospital are important to most families too. The county chosen for the study had only one-third the national average number of physicians. This is true of many rural areas.

With modern communication methods, a scarity of doctors in an area need not diminish the quality of health care. A mobile clinic in a

Video-tape equipment is an important diagnostic tool in doctorless rural areas. (Photo by Daniel Bernstein for Scientific American)

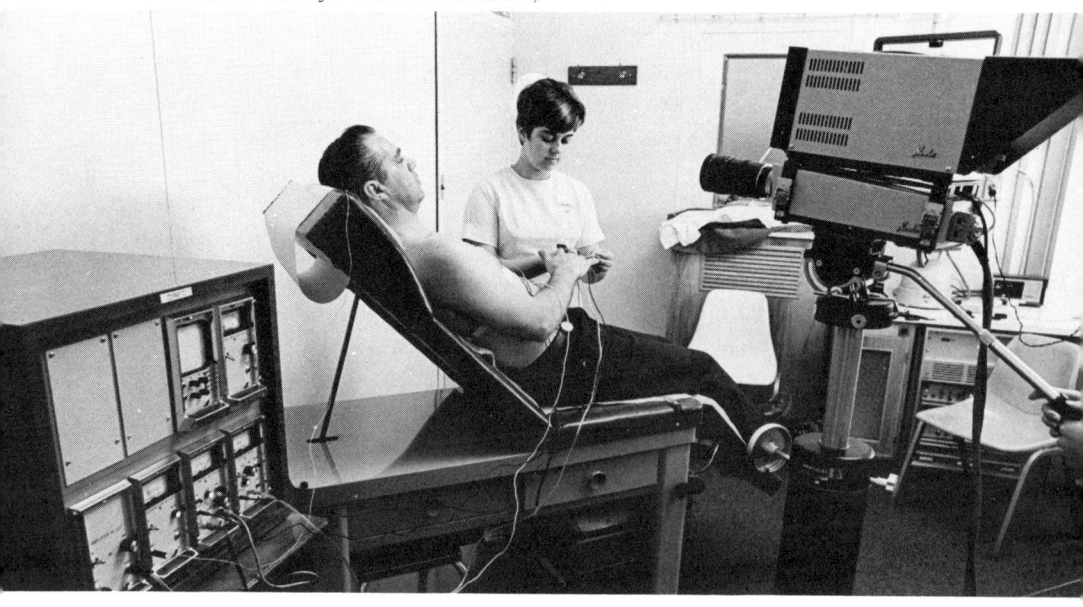

well-equipped van was used in this pilot county. It was staffed with a trained nurse and a paramedical professional. They gave inoculations and did routine examinations of schoolchildren and other groups.

Anyone who felt ill could visit the clinic or get in touch with the team by telephone. The patient described the symptoms to the nurse or paramedic. This information was recorded on tape. If the problem was more complicated than the nurse and paramedic could handle, they would contact a major city hospital.

Specialists at the hospital talked with both the patient and the clinic staff by microwave telephone. They could monitor heart action, examine eyes or run other complex tests through devices that carry signals in two directions.

The patient, without traveling more than a mile or two from home, had access to the services of a battery of medical experts in a distant city. At the same time there was warm, reassuring face-to-face contact and personal attention from the trained local staff.

A New Trend

It is too early to tell how well the pilot program will succeed in persuading businesses and families to move to the rural county that is being studied. But while the study was under way, a new trend developed in population movement.

Not many years ago hundreds of pleasant small towns were losing population and were threatened with disintegration. At the same time dozens of cities were crowded beyond their capacity to provide safe, healthful and satisfying living environments for their citizens.

In the 1960s groups of young people all over the United States began to choose to live in rural settings. Some made the move as single families. Others went in groups, to work together cooperatively on communes. They did not wait for the assurance of better jobs, special health care or all the comforts of city life. They made do with what they found, often creating their own jobs.

By 1975 this movement out of the major cities had grown to numbers that were noticeable in census samplings. It seems that the rejuvenation of small-town living might have a real impact on communities of tomorrow. But it is only one of several possibilities, as we shall see.

THE STRUCTURE OF CITIES

Cities are communities that have developed the largest and most obvious problems. So it is cities that are getting the most careful study.

A city may be compared to a living creature. The buildings provide the skeleton with steel, concrete, stone and brick for bones and some wood for cartilage. The transportation system is the life blood flowing through the "veins and arteries" of its streets and highways. Communication systems are the sensory organs through which the city sees, hears and reaches out to touch the world. People are the ever-changing, ever-in-motion, constantly renewed living cells of the city.

In ancient and medieval times, some cities grew up around a fortress or a castle located on a hilltop. From that pulsing heart a tangle of narrow, twisting lanes spread out. Other towns began as army bases to guard some frontier. When these new towns were located on level ground, the orderly military minds of their founders favored rigid patterns of rectangles for the streets, as neat as a checkerboard. Occasionally streets would radiate out like spokes of a wheel from the center—a castle, market square or church. Open space was provided for the markets, festivals and other gatherings.

When the North American continent was settled, many towns started from clusters of huts around trading posts or meetinghouses at a river landing or seashore. The first streets followed old Indian trails, cow paths or wagon routes, curving to avoid big trees or small hillocks. Some of these grew to be the main avenues of cities, named Broadway or Main Street or King's Highway.

When towns began to be planned consciously, the settlers usually thought back to their hometowns. They often laid out their towns with a church or courthouse in a square or "commons" at the center and the streets in the familiar rectangular grids.

Streets for Automobiles

Most early streets were fairly narrow, which was satisfactory until automobile traffic became congested during the first half of the twentieth century. Then wider roadways were essential.

Widening streets often involved cutting down rows of trees that had provided shade and pleasant greenery. It meant the destruction of small stretches of grassy lawn in front of many homes. Neighborhoods where this happened lost much of their attractiveness.

Increasing truck and automobile traffic had many unfortunate effects. The city streets became noisy, thick with noxious fumes and hazardous to both pedestrians and riders. As the streets were made wider and straighter, more cars filled them, moving at faster speeds. When the streets were planned for automobiles, they became less congenial for people.

Modern city planners are working to overcome these problems. One tradition that has fallen into disfavor among many planners is the checkerboard of straight streets.

All Sorts of Streets

New cities planned for the world of tomorrow will rarely have regular grids of streets running at right angles to one another. There will be a wide variety of street patterns to serve different needs.

At least one *major highway* is needed to connect any town or city with the outside world. There must be entrances and exits leading to and from this primary highway. Generally one reaches the entrances by way of on ramps leading from a secondary access road. At an exit, one follows an off ramp back to another access road. These access roads carry cars from the high-speed highway to the quieter streets where the speed of travel is strictly controlled.

From the access road one moves onto one of the collector roads that form a network through the city. These are service streets. Buses may travel down them, serving the auto-free neighborhoods.

Most homes in new communities are situated so that they face away from the collector streets. Some are set along gently curving, tree-lined ways. These curvilinear streets were the first departure from the old straight-line grid city plans. Early in the twentieth century a few model suburbs were laid out with curvilinear streets.

Interestingly, back in the fifteenth-century Italy a leading architect had the same idea. He recommended that small towns should be laid out with winding streets for greater beauty. Today curving streets do more than to break up the monotony of straight lines; they also slow traffic and are therefore safer.

Still safer for pedestrians, quieter and more pleasant for living are streets that draw no four-wheeled through traffic at all. These may be *loops* or *cul-de-sacs*. A loop street curves back from a main collector street in a semicircle and rejoins the same main street.

Usually rows of houses face the loop road from both sides. Occasionally the center of the loop is maintained as an open green space. Many of these pleasant stretches, called *maidans*, of trees and grass can be seen in New Delhi, India, which was laid out before World War I by imaginative British planners.

Grass and trees do more for a city than look pleasant. They also give off oxygen. This helps to balance the huge amounts of carbon dioxide human beings breathe out and the carbon monoxide from automobile exhausts. Plants also give off moisture, which absorbs heat as it evaporates and helps cool the air. In addition, plants absorb sound. Plantings in a city thus benefit the noise-battered ear as well as delighting the eye and the nose.

A short dead-end street that draws no through traffic at all is a cul-de-sac, which means "bottom of the bag" in French. Pedestrian walkways and bikeways may curve away from the cul-de-sac, through plantings of trees and shrubs to reach shopping centers, schools and recreation areas, without any contact with automobile traffic.

Cluster Planning

Homes are as varied in new communities as the streets. To some people the word "home" calls to mind a single-family house on its

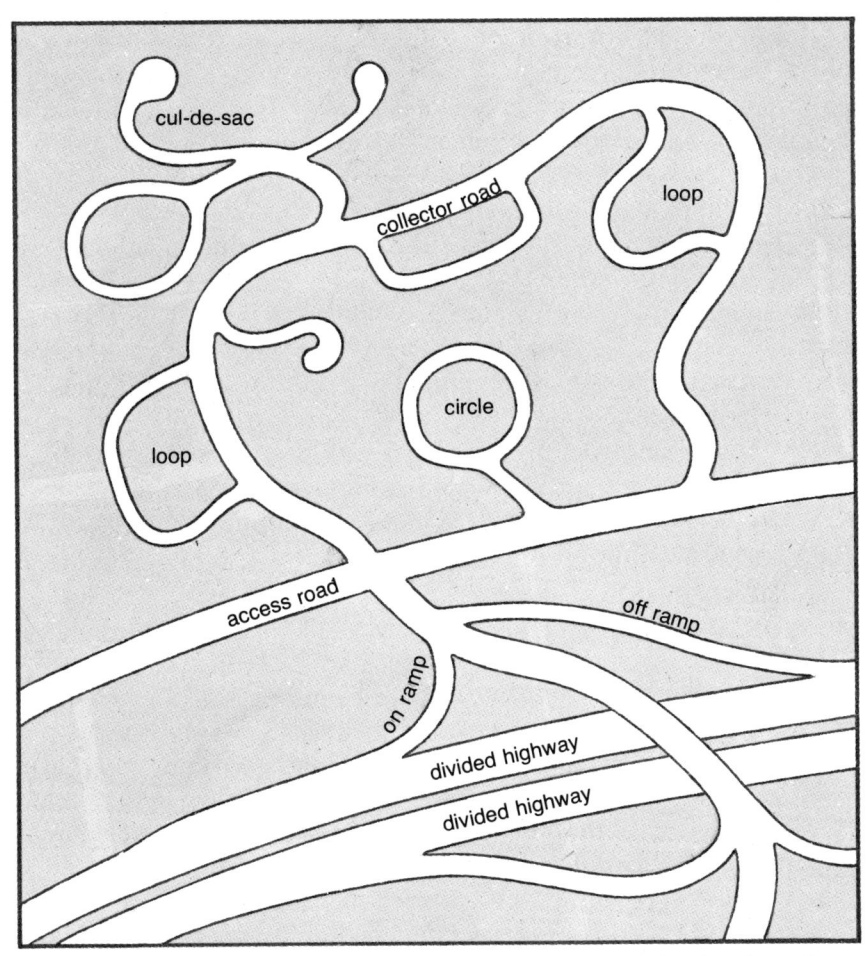

New communities feature a variety of street patterns, designed to provide safe and quiet living areas with easy access to main thoroughfares.

own plot of ground. New cities that are planned for open countryside where there is plenty of room generally provide many single-family houses. They are not always placed in the middle of the lots, as used to be the case. Today there is a trend toward smaller private lots and more open space shared by everyone.

In some luxury developments all the building lots adjoin a golf course. Each owner cedes part of the lot to the course, thus providing all the neighbors with a wide-open green space and pleasant views of grass and trees.

Homeowners with small lots place their houses at one side of the plot instead of in the center. All the free space is pulled together into one usable area at the other side of the plot. This appeals to many people more than having a useless narrow fringe of land all around the house—a border of unflavored "bun" around a "houseburger."

Two owners may back their houses up to each other along a lot line. Their garden plots then face the gardens of their neighbors on the far sides.

Two houses may even be joined together as a duplex. Or three or more houses may be joined in a row. These row houses are sometimes known as townhouses, since they used to be found only in closely built cities.

The owners of townhouses may share the expenses of gardening and outside maintenance through paying dues into a homeowners' association. This kind of small community within a community is called a condominium.

Apartment Living

As the world becomes more crowded, more families make their homes in apartment buildings. Sometimes the family owns an apartment in a building run as a condominium or a cooperative. In a condominium, each family owns its own unit. In a cooperative, each owner has a share of the whole building. In both cases, owners pay a monthly fee for maintenance.

Even in some Communist countries, such as the U.S.S.R. and Romania, where private ownership is discouraged, cooperative apartments have been growing in popularity in the 1970s. The governments offer loans at very low interest for people who want to buy apartments.

Apartment buildings are of many sorts. They may be two or three floors tall, with stairways leading to the upper levels. These *low-rise* buildings are often found in suburban areas. When each unit has a view of a green area or a private patio, they are called garden apartments.

Medium-rise buildings have four to six floors, usually with an elevator. Buildings of more than six floors are called high-rise. They almost always have elevators unless, as in the case of Hong Kong's large resettlement blocks, building costs must be kept very low.

Many flights of stairs must be climbed in some Hong Kong resettlement buildings.

Inside-Out Buildings

Elevators made tall buildings practical. Now air-conditioning has led to another development—the inside-out building. Some of these are low, sprawling shopping centers. They offer blocks of shops with show windows fronting on broad walkways. Shop doors are open in welcome because the temperature is equal inside and out. Fountains and bright patches of flowering plants decorate the walkways. Shoppers can rest on benches or in restaurants and snack shops, sheltered from the weather.

These covered shopping centers are not a new idea. For hundreds of years every sizable Middle Eastern city has had a covered bazaar. A covered bazaar usually holds acres of small shops, row on row. Many shops are very small, with raised floors on which the shop-keeper sits crosslegged to chat with customers. One can wander for hours in a bazaar, watching the men at work. In one shop, block printers stamp multicolored patterns on cloth. Farther along metalworkers hammer out bowls, trays and jugs. Along another lane, goldsmiths shape delicate jewelry or offer gold teeth stacked in small glass tumblers. Stop to consider a purchase, and the shop-keeper, with a clap of his hands, will send a lad scurrying off for small cups of sweet coffee or mint tea.

Mediterranean and South American cities have had more shopping arcades than cities in northern Europe and North America. Japan has many underground shopping areas that stretch for blocks. Until recently shops that face into buildings rather than onto a street have been found only in hotel lobbies and railway stations in the United States.

Another shopping-area innovation is the towering multi-use buildings. One of these mid-city towers offers as many shops as a sprawling suburban center. Food, clothing, toys, appliances and all sorts of specialties can be found. In addition, the upper floors feature apartments, office space, hotel rooms and even some factory work space. Art galleries, theaters, rapid-transit stations, swimming pools and ice-skating rinks will be included in many. There may also be schools for the children who live in the apartments and clinics for health care. At the center of these "inside-out" buildings there are to be large open spaces that will house airy courtyard gardens.

Apartment high-rises with shop clusters in Riga, Latvia.

Looking Out and Forward

Some architects favor building huge multi-use structures even in the open countryside. Here inside-out buildings are unnecessary. Huge all-purpose buildings can be designed so that everyone in them has a view out across open space. Each office or living unit will have a balcony or terrace jutting out at a different angle, offering outdoor living with a little privacy. Heating, lighting, air-conditioning equipment and elevators will be at the center of these compact "beehive cities." And when a city dweller wants a change of scene, open country will be close at hand.

In planning buildings for tomorrow, architects face many challenges. Most people want some privacy. They also want fresh air and contact with nature. At the same time, they want all the conveniences of city life close at hand. These individual wishes form one set of challenges. Another set has to do with conserving natural resources and energy.

The lighting, heating or cooling of buildings, providing elevator service and powering electrical devices used half of all the energy consumed in the United States in 1975. Most of that energy was produced by burning precious, irreplaceable fuel.

A great deal of electricity—and fuel—can be saved by careful planning. The amount of heat needed, even where winters are cold, can be sharply cut by using good insulating materials like concrete with air bubbles blown into it, blankets of fiber glass, rock wool, or by a sandwich filling of dry air locked between two pieces of glass. Solar-heat collectors on rooftops can trap the sun's energy for heat.

The amount of summer cooling needed can be sharply reduced by shielding windows from hot sun with roof overhangs, deep window frames or glass slanted away from the sun. Reflective glass also cuts down the amount of heat that comes into rooms.

Other economies are available: windmills to generate electric power, chemical toilets to save scarce water and dome-shaped buildings to save building materials.

Shortage of energy and resources could spur the rebirth of our cities, but this cannot be left to chance. Let us see some of the plans that are under way for more livable communities of tomorrow.

TO PLAN A PROJECT

Truck gears grind noisily; taxi horns blare. Buses lumber slowly through crowded streets as traffic fumes thicken in the trapped air. Construction drills rasp. Pedestrians shoulder their way tensely along the sidewalks. This is the situation in many urban business centers. Any reader who lives in the central part of a big city can probably add a pet annoyance to the list.

Crowding, noise and air pollution have led many businesses and shoppers to prefer suburban areas. As a result of this trend, some central business sections are now less crowded but more dismal. Empty show windows of abandoned shops gather dust and grime. Buildings fall into disrepair. Jobless would-be workers loiter on street corners.

These decaying neighborhoods usually include apartment buildings where families live crowded into small rooms, with paint peeling from walls, pipes leaking, plumbing out of repair and noxious fumes filling hallways.

People who live in surroundings like these can feel no pride in their homes. They are not concerned about the upkeep of the buildings. Windows are broken, steps crumble to a dangerous state, refuse clutters the halls and doorways.

The streets, which are the children's only playgrounds, are filthy and dangerous. People trapped by poverty in these areas become resentful of a world that is full of riches but that offers them so little.

For better or worse, these inner-city neighborhoods remain part of the skeleton of the city. If nothing is done about them, they do not just go away. Instead the problems grow and fester. And these are not merely problems of falling property values. The health and mental well-being of families and their attitudes toward the world are at stake. In a long-range sense the health and safety of the whole city and nation are endangered by urban decay.

Housing Developments

Early urban redevelopment projects after World War II often dealt with decay by razing whole slum blocks. Then the rows of four- or five-story buildings were replaced with clusters of tall, stark towers. Planners were often discouraged to find that hoodlums made life in these huge housing projects miserable for the tenants. Gangs of youths smashed hall lights and windows, tampered with elevators and made the buildings practically unlivable. The outdoor plots that were supposed to be lawns and playgrounds were soon trampled into mud and scattered with papers, cans and bottles.

Some of these multimillion-dollar projects were actually abandoned by tenants after a few years. The buildings were dynamited and razed to the ground. They had failed because there was no sense of community living.

Occasionally city officials consulted with the people who lived in one of these developments. The officials learned something about planning. They learned, for example, that having the entrances face a well-lighted courtyard could cut down on crime. Tenants could effectively keep track of comings and goings from windows overlooking the entrances.

In a housing development in Boston, the tenants asked to take over the management. When they had work to do together and real responsibility, they developed the sense of community that had been missing. They had a real stake in the success of the project. Committees of tenants patrolled the hallways and grounds in uniforms of their own choosing. Other committees tended the lawns and planted flowers where only mud and rubbish had been. Halls were cleaned and people felt more interest in keeping their own apartments in better shape. Crime dropped and contentment rose.

Block Associations

Another example of community spirit developed on the west side of Chicago. Most of the homes in a run-down area of two-flat houses were being bought by the tenants in one of the two flats. These owners had been charged inflated prices for their houses. They had a hard time keeping up payments. There was no money left in their budgets for improvements, and the whole area showed their discouragement.

Then one block, under a spirited and trained young leader, decided to get people together to do something. The property owners formed a block association and met in homes to make plans. Each family put a few dollars into the community fund. Some of the men worked in the construction industry—one as a sand blaster, another as a carpenter, a third as a cement worker. They showed their neighbors how to patch and clean their house walls and sidewalks. Another neighbor who knew something about landscaping supervised filling holes in neglected front lawns with good soil and a layer of sod bought from the community fund.

Every homeowner, spurred by the rising spirits, managed to buy a standing lantern for one corner of the front lawn. These matching lanterns gave the block a touch of elegance and made it one of the best lighted (and thus one of the safest) areas of the city.

Two vacant lots were turned into a small park, with a wading pool for small children, a basketball court for larger ones and a grassy picnic area.

The Chicago Police Department, impressed by the work, provided traffic signs and pavement "bumps" to slow the traffic, since the long block had 200 children. And they re-established foot patrols to keep the community safe.

Strong community spirit is the most important ingredient in the renovation of certain city streets. (Photo by Stuart Fischer)

All these developments attracted the attention of the neighborhood. Other blocks, inspired by this example, organized block associations and went to work to improve their own surroundings.

Follow the Leader

The key to action is having a leader to get things started. More colleges and universities are developing courses in community planning, environmental sciences and urban studies. The name of any course is not important; what is important is the training of young people to deal as leaders with the problems of cities.

Many skills are needed; engineers, construction workers, designers, draftsmen, structural and landscape architects, sociologists, political scientists and teachers must work together. Some projects involve not just one small area but a whole city.

To Start a Plan

How does a whole city "pull itself up by its bootstraps" while it is still wearing the boots? First there has to be widespread concern about solving the problems. Then there has to be professional leadership. Usually a private foundation or a government agency provides funds to pay for a study by a team of urban planners.

One study of this kind was undertaken in Cleveland, Ohio. Since the goal was not merely to rebuild the skeleton of the city or just to modernize the streets and transit system but to provide a satisfying living place for people, the professionals started work by consulting the people of the city. They assembled a sampling of businessmen, working people, public officials, housewives and students to participate in an idea workshop.

The group was asked to take a six-mile walk through the downtown area. As they walked, people took down notes. They were all familiar with the problems of their city, but now their observations were sharpened by a fresh sense of purpose.

The problems were common ones. The central business district had once been beautiful, located on the shore of one of the Great Lakes. Now it was one of the most dismally rundown in the country. Most of the people with money and influence had moved out of the city into the surrounding suburbs. Each suburb set up a local government and collected taxes from its residents to support its own activities. Many wage earners commuted into the city to work and depended on it for income, but the city taxes they paid were small. The tax base of the city shrank as its needs grew.

Schools and other services deteriorated. Police cars broke down on their rounds for lack of repairs. Violence surged up recurrently. Many low-income families were trapped in dreary neighborhoods. They had no transportation to reach jobs that might be available. Many did not have the proper education to qualify for jobs even if they could reach them.

Everyone gathered for the urban-planning workshop was aware of all this; almost all of them were deeply dissatisfied with what had become of their city. But they did not see what they could do. As one of the professional urban planners said, they "seem to have an inferiority complex about their city."

Following the tour of the downtown area, the group gathered in a conference room for an idea session. The discussion was lively. There was plenty of difference of viewpoint and opinion. But disagreement often sharpened the thinking and led to new ideas. Out of the session came a list of points on which almost everyone agreed.

Recreation areas are a prime need for young people in urban areas. (Photo by Stuart Fischer)

Many of them apply to most decaying urban centers. These were the key points:

Downtown should be planned as a place for people, not just for business and real-estate interests.

New housing is needed in the central city, much of it low-cost, for low-income families. But the housing in any neighborhood should attract people of different income levels and backgrounds. (On this point there was especially lively disagreement.)

Public buildings and facilities such as libraries, museums, theaters and concert halls should be conveniently scattered throughout the city.

Public transportation must be improved, not just by the addition of more buses but by some major new system such as a monorail. (Cleveland has one rapid-transit line serving the airport.) Water service on the lake front and up the river might be explored.

Recreation is a prime need, especially for young people. Sports and hobby programs, free concerts and theater performances are needed. Vacant lots or parking areas should be converted to recreational use. Some unused land could be divided into garden plots.

The lake front and river front have great recreation potential. Pollution must end and these once-attractive areas developed for living and recreation.

The planners taped the discussion so that they would not miss any of the suggestions. Some of the ideas were beyond the range of probable achievement, but many were both original and practical.

Back in their office, the planners went to work with slide rules and computers, shelves of reference books on economics and government, real-estate figures and school and employment reports. Months of work lay ahead before the urban-renewal plan would take shape. And then to put the plan into action would require more months of lining up public support, for a project that could upgrade the whole central city would be immensely expensive. Funds would be available only if officials could be made to feel the importance of the project to themselves and all the citizens of a warmly concerned community.

NEW HEARTS FOR OLD CITIES

World War II left in ruins many cities of Europe, the Soviet Union, Japan and other lands. Large-scale rebuilding was urgently needed. So these areas led the way in planning new life for old central cities. Many different approaches were used.

One way to restore an old city is to rebuild everything as it was in its great days. This is what the people of Warsaw, the proud old capital of Poland, did. Warsaw had been almost completely destroyed by the Nazi armies. The Polish people, with great devotion and perseverance, rebuilt their capital city, house by house, building by building, as it had been before the war.

In the heart of Warsaw had been a paved open square surrounded by tall old gabled houses dating back to medieval times. Every painted gable facing the square was painstakingly reconstructed, though some modern conveniences were added inside the buildings. Handsome seventeenth- and eighteenth-century palaces and other fine buildings were reconstructed by using old paintings as guides.

The principal cities of the Soviet Union also were in ruins at the end of World War II. As a result, the Soviet Union has undertaken the world's most massive urban reconstruction program. Here the approach is quite different from Poland's. The style and size of the principal new buildings are as huge in scale as the whole project.

Government buildings in the capitals of several Soviet republics—for example, Minsk, the capital of Byleorussia, and

Capitol of the Ukrainian SSR in Kiev.

Kiev, capital of the Ukraine—are immense in scale and more impressive for size than beauty.

Most of the new housing in the Soviet Union is also in huge new developments of high-rise apartment buildings. Groups of these buildings, each containing thousands of apartments, are under construction almost constantly. Huge cranes lift prefabricated units into place like stacks of empty cardboard boxes. The buildings are not always well constructed, but the increase in the number of family units of housing in the Soviet Union in the past thirty years is impressive.

Each cluster of apartment buildings includes a low-built section containing shops, a theater and a coffee shop or restaurant. There is usually a school and a health clinic nearby. And there is certain to be some open space.

39

In the center of a Soviet city there is always a park. The parks are outstanding both in numbers and in size. These parks reflect the government's philosophy, which teaches common sharing as opposed to private ownership. The parks are the "front lawns" or "back gardens" for all the city people who make their homes in small, cramped apartments. Children play there, oldsters visit, have a snack in a café or read posted newspapers. Parks are important parts of Soviet communities.

Most of the new Soviet apartment complexes are built at the edges of cities. But Sweden's capital has an impressive urban redevelopment project in the middle of the city.

Stockholm is a beautiful seaport city that was not damaged by the war. Narrow lanes lined with tall houses climb a seaside hill at its heart. Ships and boats dock cozily alongside some of the principal streets. The Swedish people are interested in all sorts of modern design, from fabrics to pottery to automobiles to cities. So it is not surprising that Stockholm boasts an outstandingly handsome modern cluster of white high-rise buildings ranging from five to eighteen stories in height.

The buildings are joined by a pedestrian mall lined with attractive shops. Restaurants, theaters and supervised play areas where mothers can leave small children for a few hours are located near the apartments. Good public transportation, including subway service, is available. Families can travel swiftly and easily from the heart of modern Stockholm to the suburbs or countryside.

Cities within Cities

Stockholm's central project approaches the ideal of "city within a city" projects.

London, capital of Great Britain, was severely damaged by bombing during World War II. In repairing this destruction, London's planners pioneered the "city within a city" idea. Their reconstruction projects were called "new towns." These were really large neighborhoods, each planned to house as many as 100,000 people.

The English new towns were planned to provide more than improved housing for people, many of whom had lived in slums before. They were to offer even more than the Soviet apartment complexes. The London new towns would contain factories, work-

Modern high-rise buildings in Stockholm are connected by a shop-lined pedestrian mall.

shops, offices and other employement opportunities as well as small shops, theaters and cafés. Residents would live near their work and save travel time and expenses.

This ideal has not been completely successful. The English working people had specific ideas about where they wanted to live, regardless of where they worked. Even if they changed jobs, they did not always want to move their families.

This is only one of several kinds of problems that have beset the city-within-a city projects. A redevelopment plan on the Montparnasse in Paris has been criticized by the French for several reasons: transportation had not been well planned and there was not enough space for sunlight and greenery. It was another instance of the planners overlooking the needs of the residents of the project.

Rising costs can cause difficulties too, particularly in countries like the United States, where groups of private investors rather than the governments do the financing.

Some dream plans have foundered for financial reasons. Battery Park, a city-within-a city planned for 100 acres of landfill along New York City's Hudson River, was to have 21,000 apartments and nearly five million feet of office space, hotels, shops, parks and other recreational facilities. Roadways for vehicles and public transportation were designed for underground. Walkways were to be free of vehicular traffic. But this dream has not yet materialized because of financing difficulties. An East River project on Roosevelt Island has fared better. Some families have moved in, and an aerial tramway to Manhattan has been built.

Others have started more modestly with existing buildings. One of these projects began when a small group of citizens became interested in a small riverbank area near the heart of Minneapolis.

A neighborhood of simple one- and two-story homes had become badly run down. Many families had moved out and most of the shops were boarded up. About 4,000 inhabitants had stayed on and did not want to leave.

The area had advantages that were not being utilized. There were a campus of the state university, two small colleges and two major hospitals. These were a potential source of educational and professional groups who might return to live in the area if it could be made more attractive.

A group of small investors began to buy up pieces of the rundown property. They repaired one building at a time, taking care to resettle any tenants they displaced. Renters in the newly repaired buildings were encouraged to express themselves. Soon there were flower-bright houses and handicraft shops galore. Experimental theaters appeared, and a lively feeling developed as people became involved in their community.

This small-scale project prospered so pleasantly that it inspired a large-scale "city-within-a-city" plan for the whole area. At this stage government assistance was requested for the costly twenty-year plan.

Plans for the new mini-city in Minneapolis include high-rise apartments of thirty to forty stories with covered walkways above the street traffic to connect the buildings. Medium-rise apartments and other business buildings are planned, too, along with a center for the performing arts. Schools, playgrounds, river-front parks and a handsome central square will complete the community, which is planned eventually to house 30,000 people. The first new apartments and shops have been occupied for some time. Whether the plan will be completed as it has been envisioned depends principally on the availability of financial backing. Even the most splendid dream must have practical roots if it is to come true.

Up with the Downtown

The move of prosperous families to the suburbs and the growth of suburban shopping centers have spelled disaster for many downtown areas. Recently, though, more attention has turned to revitalizing the hearts of old cities.

Some urban planners feel that this reconstruction is the hope of the future. The new cities are in the main having a hard time remaining viable. Many of the planned satellite communities have been knocked out by difficult financial conditions. The downtown reconstruction projects can draw on the business community, which has a stake in maintaining the area, for support.

At least 92 U.S. cities have joined an international downtown association that shares experiences and ideas. Some dramatic results have been achieved.

Gas-lighted streets lead to colorful shops and popular restaurants in an area along the Chicago River that had been abandoned to decay not many years ago. Water taxis speed along a parklike stretch of the river in San Antonio. A beautiful St. Louis redevelopment project with a river-front recreation area has been built facing the Mississippi. Los Angeles has constructed a handsome new civic center with theaters, parks, fountains and public buildings close to the city's revitalized financial district. Denver's Technological Center is turning an underdeveloped area into a showplace for skyscrapers.

Even enthusiasts agree that these plans lack sufficient low-cost housing. As long as major projects are privately financed for profit, the poor will be neglected. If we are to have a healthy and just society, this is an oversight that must be corrected. Any worthy dream for the city of tomorrow must include workable and healthful housing for all.

SUBURBS, SATELLITES, NEW CITIES

When a city becomes too crowded for comfort, what is to be done? In ancient Greece, a shipload of citizens would sail away to found a new city. In the first half of the twentieth century families moved to the suburbs, and the wage-earners commuted to the city every working day. After World War II whole new communities developed beyond the suburbs. Since life in these communities still revolves around the nearby city, they are often called satellites.

Some Satellites

One of the earliest and most attractive of the satellite communities is Tapiola, the "garden city" located quite near the capital city of Helsinki in Finland. The name Tapiola comes from the legendary home of the forest folk in Finland's ancient epic poem *The Kalevala*. And the city named for the legend is appropriately set in the woodlands.

At Tapiola's center is a cluster of white towers encircling a paved plaza that forms the business heart of the community. Low apartment buildings face tree-lined streets that curve out from the plaza. Radiating beyond these are a circle of two-story row houses. On the outskirts are small, neat single-family dwellings scattered in groves of trees.

Tapiola is within easy commuting distance of Helsinki and is closer to being a suburb than an independent city. It is difficult for new communities to remain independent of the well-established parent cities.

Yugoslavia's capital city of Belgrade is living with one of the problems common to many satellite communities. The heart of Belgrade was heavily bombed during World War II. When peace came, the government faced the double challenge of rebuilding the old capital and planning for population growth.

Some handsome modern buildings now stand in the demolished areas of the old central city. To provide for the growing population, government planners decided to establish a new satellite city.

Belgrade stands on the point where the River Sava flows into the Danube. The old city is on one side of the Sava. It was decided to build the satellite city across the river.

The principal buildings of the Yugoslavian government are set in a spacious park on the bank of the Danube in New Town. Of the new city's land, 40 percent was allotted for parks. Housing for 100,000 people was planned in high-rise apartments not far away, surrounded by green space. There were to be factories and offices to provide employment.

Open space in the civic center of Tapiola, Finland.

Things did not work out as the developers planned, though. Only about one-fifth of the workers who live in the new city also work there. The other workers cross the river to the old city and back home again each work day. There are not many bridges, so traffic is congested during rush hours.

Locating business and industry near residential neighborhoods promises several benefits. It cuts down travel time for workers whose jobs are close to their homes. They have more free time to spend with their families and for recreation. In addition, the streets will be used both during the work day and leisure time. They will not be like the streets of many downtown areas that are crowded during work hours and empty at night. At least that is the plan!

To Plan a Satellite

To speak of new satellite cities as completed projects is to skip over years in planning, financing and construction. A closer look at one such project will tell us something about the care with which the planners must proceed.

The broad express highway leading toward the Pacific Coast northwest of Los Angeles cuts through rolling hills. They are green after winter rains and tawny-gold during the long dry summers. Not many years ago cattle grazed on the broad rangelands, and horses were pastured in the meadows, shaded by live oaks.

In the last twenty years the fringes of the city have crept farther out across these valleys. High-speed highways have made it possible to commute long distances into the city to work. Land developers bought up many wide meadows, laid curving roads through them and lined the roads with houses built for quick sales.

Some people worried as they saw open grasslands disappear under blacktop roads and close-built roofs. At rush hours the highways were soon as packed with cars as any city streets.

Still more housing tracts went up. More lanes were added to the highways. But the rush-hour traffic was never lessened because home building proceeded faster than the widening of highways.

The solution to the urban sprawl that was ruining the countryside seemed to be in more careful planning. These planned communities would provide employment opportunities that would eliminate most of the commuting that crowds the highways.

Building a whole planned community takes much more land than a cluster of new houses. Early in the 1960s one group of planners found that a ranch of nearly 12,000 acres about forty miles from downtown Los Angeles was on the market. This land seemed to be an almost perfect setting for a new, planned community. The project would really be a satellite city, located between a major city and a splendid recreation area along the Pacific coast.

There were broad, fairly level acres for easy building. These acres were dotted with fine old oaks that the developers were determined to preserve wherever possible. In the south a range of pleasant foot hills rested below rugged mountains. These hills and mountains provided a beautiful background and a protected recreation area for future homeowners.

Before the land was purchased the master plans for the area had to be considered. Roads, schools, sewage disposal, fire protection, water supply and taxation were some of the matters that had to be checked. The property spanned a county line, so two county governments had to approve the plans for the development.

The first agreement signed with the two counties provided that the new community, to be called Westlake Village, could be built to hold about 70,000 people. Before many people had moved in, zoning rules for the area were changed. It was feared that the whole region was going to be overcrowded. So the plan was cut back to an eventual population of about 50,000 people on the 12,000 acres.

The developers were concerned about this zoning change. It meant that more of the overhead cost of building roads, installing utilities and landscaping would have to be divided among 50,000 people instead of 70,000. This would make each unit more expensive. Also, early experience with satellite cities—in England after World War II, for example—had shown that larger communities were more likely to succeed than smaller ones.

Planning for the Future

By the time the zoning change was made, a great deal of money had been invested in the project. The land had been bought for tens of millions of dollars. The whole area had to be made ready for the building of homes, apartments, schools, shopping and business centers, a community hospital, recreation areas such as golf courses, tennis courts and riding trails and enough light industries and major business offices to employ many of the homeowners.

The first major construction project was a dam that was planned to store natural drainage waters in a man-made lake. Many of the city's home sites were planned to face the curving lakeshore.

The lake bed had to be dredged and all the utilities for the homesites installed before building could be started. All electric and telephone wiring had to be buried underground. Sewers and storm drains were installed. Roadways were laid out to link all the neighborhoods. There was a great deal of work for engineers.

Marketing experts had to survey the surrounding area to estimate how many people might shop in the stores of the new community. They also needed to know how many people nearby could be counted on to work in shops and offices here. And experts in real estate had to figure out the size and number of single-family houses and garden apartments the new city should have.

Columbia, Maryland is one of the most successful planned cities in the country. To be completed by 1980, it is expected to have a population of 110,000. The town center features buildings of an urban character but is easily accessible to the surrounding housing areas.

Money for land, preliminary expenses, salaries and, finally, construction costs were poured into this project for more than three years before the first house was sold. This long-range financing has proved to be a great problem for the developers of many satellite communities. As prices rose and the purchasing of new homes became more difficult, some developers have gone bankrupt. Satellite cities have been more successful in countries where the government finances the whole project.

A government body can build apartments for low-income families without expecting the low rents to pay for the buildings. Private investors cannot earn back their money with low rents. The community we have been discussing could not, for this reason, have low-rent apartments. The planners had to try to get their investors a fair return on their investment.

There are many problems involved in planning and constructing a new community. But within three years of the purchase of the land, the first homeowners were moving into houses and apartments looking out onto green lawns and a golf course. Shops were opening in the shaded shopping centers. Sailboats dotted the man-made lake. Within another three years a large insurance company, electronic plants and automobile dealers were keeping hundreds of people busy in the satellite's industrial park.

This new community had existed only on the drawing boards a few years before but now it began to have a life of its own.

2 TRANSPORTATION:

How Wide a World?

The steam engine, which revolutionized transportation, did not come into use until about 200 years ago. During all the thousands of years before that, the fastest means of travel on land was by galloping horse. Top speed at sea was that of a ship running full sail before a brisk breeze.

Until the early nineteenth century most people traveled at a considerably slower pace than those top limits and did not venture very far at any speed. They lived in or near small rural villages where open-air markets were held once a week. The market provided the few items that most farm families could not grow or make for themselves.

Travel was largely limited to an occasional visit to a neighboring town for a wedding or other special events. Occasionally a group of people set off on a religious pilgrimage to some famous shrine. And war sometimes took the men to distant lands. But the world in which most people moved was no larger than a few miles in diameter.

Most people lived out their lives in the communities where they were born. Those who did move far away said farewell forever to all they left behind. The journey across the sea or even across the continent was a project most people could not expect to retrace within a lifetime.

The bonds that enclosed people's lives were broken by the steam engine and its offshoots. Each decade the horizons of ordinary people stretched and expanded, pushed by chugging railway trains and churning paddlewheel steamboats. During the past century the world of transportation has continued to develop and change our horizons.

The introduction of the automobile and the airplane has made quick and comfortable travel across thousands of miles possible for millions of people. In industrialized nations workers and their families plan holidays far from home, knowing that they can travel swiftly by car, bus, train, steamship or airplane.

Even in less industrialized lands, brightly painted buses rattle along country roads, crammed with passengers, luggage and goods bound for market. In some mountainous lands where roads are few, such as Ethiopia, many villagers who have never ridden in a motor-driven land vehicle casually step onto airplanes that put down on meadow clearings. Advances in transportation have been stretching our opportunities in all directions. They have permitted us to see exotic sights, to meet people of different backgrounds, to buy goods from distant lands and to sell our produce in markets far away. But at the same time that our horizons have been widening, something has been happening at the center of our lives, in the heart of many of our communities.

Today, during rush hours in many downtown areas and on the highways leaving the cities, traffic moves at a pace much slower than the speed of a healthy trotting horse. And even a horse would not stay healthy for long, breathing in the air that is polluted by the fumes exhaled from buses, trucks, taxis and private cars. People stalled in traffic have come to realize that if our world is to continue to be a pleasant place to live, great improvements must be made, particularly in urban transportation.

THE AUTOMOBILE CITY

Today we take for granted many things that had not been dreamed of when your great-grandparents were young. Parking meters along the sidewalks; multistoried garages and black-topped parking lots like toothless holes in business blocks; clustered shopping centers surrounded by acres of paved space for cars—all these are commonplace in and around today's cities. We are accustomed to drive-in theaters, restaurants, banks and other businesses. We scarcely give a thought to service stations with rows of pumps, to drive-through car washes, tow trucks, ambulances with screaming sirens, used-car lots and automotive junkyards. Multilevel expressways stretch across former farmlands in endless ribbons tied into complex clover-leaf bows at interchanges. All these by-products of the automobile age are now very familiar to us. But to our grandchildren, today's modes of transportation will seem as quaint and strange and old-fashioned as the pre-automobile world seems to us. Transportation is now at the dawn of another important new era.

The Good Old Days

Before the automobile came to dominate life, particularly in the United States, most people lived close to their work. In small towns almost everyone could walk to school, to the shops and markets and to work.

As towns grew into cities, public transportation was provided. But for some years it, too, moved at the speed of a walk—usually that of a walking horse. It was in 1831 that the first horse-drawn streetcars were put into service in New York City. During the nineteenth century horse-drawn and, later, electric-powered trolley cars became common sights on the streets of towns and cities.

Even small towns had trolley tracks laid on the main streets. Almost everyone lived within an easy walk of the trolley line. Neighborhoods developed along these routes. With the use of perhaps one transfer, a person could ride to the central business district or almost anywhere else in town.

When someone was making an out-of-town trip, the trolley was used to get to the railway station. Factories were built near the railway tracks so the goods could easily be loaded onto the trains for shipping. Trolleys ran close to the factories. Many workers lived close to the factories, but they would use the trolleys for errands or outings.

Railways also provided special passenger train service to nearby communities. As a result of this convenient train service, many well-to-do families moved out of cities to suburban communities. For example, a whole series of pleasant towns grew up along the railway west of Philadelphia. This area, known as the Main Line, became the socially smart place for Philadelphians to live during the latter half of the nineteenth century. The same was true of Chicago's North Shore suburbs, which were served by the Chicago & Northwestern Railway. Rail rapid transit came to Boston in 1829 and to New York's Long Island communities a few years later. Railways encouraged the first movement to the fashionable suburbs. The next great wave was created by another new form of transportation.

The Early Automobiles

With the 1900s came the automobile. At first it was used mainly for outings and for Sunday-afternoon drives on quiet roads. Most roads in those days were of rutted dirt or gravel. They were dusty when dry and treacherously slippery when wet. Over swampy spots "corduroy roads," fashioned of logs laid crosswise side by side, often provided the basis for a bouncy ride.

Highway maps were nonexistent. Travelers had only small

The streetcar was an important mode of transportation in the U. S. until World War I.

guidebooks with directions that might read "200 yards past the schoolhouse, turn right at the red barn." Service stations did not exist. It was wise to carry an extra can of gasoline on a long trip and a picnic lunch as well, since roadside eating places were few. A motor trip of any length was almost certain to be punctuated with at least one stop for patching a flat tire.

As the number of cars increased, certain main streets and roads were designated "arterial highways." These roads were to carry the main flow of traffic much as the arteries carry blood through the body. Traffic from side streets had to yield when it reached an arterial highway, stopping at newly installed stop signs before it could cross or turn into the flow of cars.

By the late 1930s increasing numbers of workers were driving to their jobs in automobiles. Service stations and garages were built to keep all the automobiles in working order. They replaced the livery stables that had housed horse-drawn rigs and lodged privately owned horses. Hitching posts for horses disappeared from curbings, to be replaced by parking meters that kept cars from occupying spaces too long. But these were minor changes when compared to the problems that overtook communities as they became "automobile cities."

Blessing or Curse?

As automobiles became a dominant force, even the physical shape of cities began to change. As many factories began to ship their goods by truck instead of by train, they no longer had to stay in the crowded downtown sections of cities just to be near the train tracks. Plants were moved out to cheaper land in the country. The factory buildings left behind often became abandoned eyesores.

Workers' families had frequently lived in densely populated neighborhoods near the factories or mills. With the factories gone, these families moved away. The housing near abandoned factories frequently became rundown slums.

Trolleys began to be replaced by buses, which could travel without tracks and power lines. Their routes could go through all parts of the cities and to the outlying areas. Many workers began to ride buses to work when they moved to distant areas.

Bus companies tried to keep up with the scattering population. But bus lines could not go everywhere. And with increasing prosperity, workers began to drive their own automobiles to factories or offices. As long as they were going by car, it did not matter much whether their jobs—or their homes—were out in the country or in the heart of town. And there were none of the delays encountered on public transportation.

Driving to work saved a good deal of time, and it seemed the epitome of convenience and comfort. But as more people drove, the streets and roads were not wide enough to accommodate them all.

Highways were broadened from two narrow lanes to three- and then to four-lane roadways. Between major cities main routes were expanded to eight-lane divided highways. These cut through the hearts of many smaller communities, splitting neighborhoods, separating children from their schools and homes from convenient shops. Property along the noisy right-of-ways became less desirable and less valuable.

These roads, which were called expressways by highway engineers, had some level-grade crossings where traffic had to stop. Drivers on long trips became impatient with the delays caused by repeated stops for cross-traffic as they were going through towns. It was this impatience and the desire for speed that led to the freeway, the greatest innovation in route design of the automobile age.

Travel on a freeway is never interrupted for cross traffic. All cross-traffic drives on different grade levels, either below or above the main highway. A freeway has limited access; a car has to travel to an access point to enter or leave. Between these points, separate frontage roads run parallel to the main highway carrying traffic to the on and off ramps.

We take freeways for granted, but years of trial and error and study went into their development. Left turns were a major problem that had to be solved if traffic was to move smoothly, swiftly and safely. To eliminate left turns across traffic, engineers developed the sweeping clover-leaf interchanges.

Another problem was having traffic slowed by the low speed at which cars entered the freeway. Access ramps have been steadily lengthened to permit traffic to build up speed before entering the freeway lanes.

Expressways and freeways began to occupy more space in cities; and highway right-of-ways and the wide loops of interchanges stretched over more acres of farmland across the countryside. Parking lots and multistory garages multiplied. But these could solve for only a brief time the problems of making room for crowds of automobiles, in motion or at rest.

Automobile travel in and around major cities now gobbles up time in a most frustrating way. The speed of urban traffic has continued to

Highways and interchanges sprawl over the countryside near Helsinki, Finland, destroying a great deal of farmland.

inch upward, on the average. But rush-hour congestion is a serious source of irritation. The congestion has become a health hazard as well, because the drivers are breathing heavily polluted air.

Many workers long to be freed of the strain and irritation of long commutes added to both ends of the work day. But public transportation services in many areas have dwindled, if they were ever established. The wholesale switch from public transportation to private cars killed many of these services.

So for millions of people by the 1960s and early 1970s there was no satisfactory alternative to creeping slowly to work by car. Other related problems were growing. Automobiles contributed to air and noise pollution. They devoured great quantities of irreplaceable fossil fuels. And by 1972 motor-vehicle accidents in the United States killed 150 people every day and injured 11,000 more. The casualties for a single year were higher than all those suffered in the United States' longest war, while the property damage amounts to about $13.9 billion a year. And the United States' fatality rate is one of the world's lowest!

An automobile is an expensive purchase, second only to the purchase of a home in the budgets of most families. Because of planned obsolescence, most cars can be depended on to be serviceable for only a few years.

All of these automobile-related costs and problems have prompted people to examine the whole transportation picture in the "automobile city." The sharpest attention and criticism have been directed to that most extravagant form of transportation—the personal automobile for one-passenger trips.

An Object Lesson

The most vivid lessons of the automobile age are to be found in areas that have been developed largely since the age of the automobile began. Los Angeles, California, with its sprawling suburbs is a prime example. Only one hundred years ago Los Angeles was scarcely more than a mission village. Since then, a scattering of small towns set among orange groves and truck gardens have been blended together by the expanding suburbs. Together they form a megalopolis that sprawls along the Pacific coast for more than 100 miles and reaches inland as much as 65 miles.

Today many of these once-independent communities are referred to as "bedroom suburbs." Thousands of workers travel each workday morning to jobs elsewhere and at the end of the work day they commute home again. Everyone moves farther away from work to get out of the smog and by driving those extra miles twice a day helps to create still more smog.

This has not always been the case. At the turn of the century electric trolley lines were laid in Southern California as in other regions. Around Los Angeles the trolley lines were laid through bean fields to the mountains and the sea. New communities grew up along these transportation routes. And many fortunes were made from the swift rise in the value of farmland along the trolley lines.

Those rail lines continued to serve the area until the post-World War II surge in automobile ownership and daily driving. Use of the "big red cars" (as the trolleys were called) dwindled. Fares had to be raised to try to make them profitable. Higher fares encouraged more people to drive themselves. Use of the trolleys dwindled and the service was reduced. This made the lines even less attractive to the passengers who remained, and finally the routes were abandoned entirely. This sad story of the decline of public transportation in Los Angeles has been duplicated in many cities and towns.

Los Angeles in the mid-1970s is at last re-examining the need for extensive rapid public transportation. But the rights-of-way for those old trolley tracks have long since been abandoned. Acquiring new rights-of-way looms as an immense expense.

The big red cars and their tracks once linked the communities of the Los Angeles area like beads on a chain. But in the automobile age new suburbs have spread out to resemble an endless web around the network of freeways. These costly and land-gobbling freeways, used largely by one-passenger cars, form the skeleton of this sprawling automobile city.

The city no longer spreads out around one dominant central "heart." Fewer people entered the downtown business district of Los Angeles daily in 1975 than in 1929, despite a 250 percent rise in population for the area and a recent flurry of downtown skyscraper construction. Business and shopping centers have become more and more widely scattered.

In trying to plan a new public transportation system, it is impossible to draw a few simple lines between most people's homes and their places of work. In an automobile city it has not seemed important or even desirable to live near one's work. Tracing on a map the routes people in one medium-size office take to and from work would form a complex pattern. This has made it difficult even to plan car pools for commuting to work, though some pools are being organized with the help of computers. Setting up a public transportation pattern that will satisfy the needs of a large proportion of those single-occupant car drivers is much more difficult.

The New Frontier?

It seems sensible to expand those "bedroom suburbs" into well-rounded communities that can offer a wide range of occupations. About 60 percent of today's workers are employed in service industries. These include banks, utilities, insurance companies and other employers whose offices do not need to be located in congested city centers. Modern computers and communication systems can keep widely scattered offices in close touch with one another. Small branch offices already exist in many outlying communities. If this trend continues, many workers who prefer to live in suburbs or even in small rural communities should be able to work close to their homes. They could walk to work or use local bus lines instead of investing in cars that are driven only a few miles each day.

To some experts in transportation and community problems, this seems the ideal solution for many people. But the automobile is an important part of many households. It has given Americans a feeling of power and independence. They have become accustomed to being able to go wherever and whenever the mood strikes them.

In countries such as India, most people have not had this power to move about freely. A new factory or university built at the edge of an Indian city has the housing for its employees included in its plans. Factory workers, teachers and office personnel are assigned quarters in staff housing according to their earnings. They are within easy reach of their work, and families do not expect to travel far or often.

Movements to persuade workers to live as close as this to their jobs or even to "take the jobs to the workers" had little success in the United States before the mid-1970s. But the rising costs of automobiles and fuel may force people to break free, at least in part, from the tyranny of the automobile.

THE FUTURE OF THE AUTOMOBILE

Banish the automobile? The suggestion naturally fills millions of hearts with dismay. The automobile provides the most comfortable, often luxurious transportation ever devised. It offers the traveler complete flexibility of both time and direction of movement. It gives the driver a sense of power, of being in control of circumstances.

Sales of cars have been booming on every continent, even in Communist countries where private ownership is discouraged. Wherever the standard of living rises, ownership of an automobile has been a symbol of personal achievement. The larger the automobile, the brighter the success it seemed to reflect.

In many areas a whole way of life has been built up around the automobile. Almost all over the world much of the residential and business building as well as the construction of streets and highways has been slanted to accommodate automobile traffic or the probability of future traffic. Recently, though, the rumblings of protest against the misuse of today's automobiles have grown to roars.

The Case Against the Car

"The internal combustion engine is noisy, inefficient, and pollutes the atmosphere," said one environmental writer.

Another critic, writing about the center of Rome in 1973, spoke of it as "paralyzed by automania." He complained of a bedlam of squealing horns and screeching brakes at rush hours, with progress down many streets made almost impossible by double parking.

A third spoke of the slaughter and maiming of people on the highways of the world as "an international scandal."

The automobile is one of the most wasteful consumers of irreplaceable fossil fuels. With the increasing awareness of the genuine energy crisis facing the world, this has become a particularly meaningful criticism.

Supporters of the automobile point out that it has been evolving and improving constantly during all this century. They claim that these beneficial developments are proceeding more rapidly and effectively than ever. The automobile of tomorrow, its defenders say, will have outgrown its present faults. Let us see some of the directions in which this evolution is moving.

Quiet and Clean

One criticism of the automobile is that it pollutes the atmosphere with noise and exhaust fumes. Actually each individual automobile motor runs quietly enough to suit even its critics. Much of the disagreeable noise associated with automobile traffic comes from trucks and motorcycles or from improper use of horns, brakes and accelerators. These latter noises reflect the social problems caused by numbers of cars rather than a technical weakness of the average machine.

Many cities have successfully banned the use of automobile horns to cut noise pollution. Others, like Rome, whose automobile problem was mentioned previously, have tried closing the historical, shopping, and governmental areas of the city, with narrow old streets ill-suited to auto traffic. Changes in people's attitudes and driving habits are needed more urgently than technical improvements.

Heavy trucks do cause noise and traffic problems, no matter how well they are driven. Some cities have banned them from central sections during business hours. Deliveries of goods have to be made at night when traffic is lightest.

Another plan for lessening truck noise involves setting up terminals in outlying sections of the city. Long-distance haulers unload their goods at the terminal, and it is sorted by computers, according to its destination. No longer do trucks have to rumble around the city, dropping off small consignments of goods here and there. Instead each truck that leaves the suburban terminal can head straight for one destination, perhaps a single large building, where it will deliver goods that have arrived from many starting points.

The centers of a few cities are being modernized, following ambitious reconstruction plans. In some of these new cities-within-cities heavy traffic is routed underground. These tunnels have to be carefully engineered and expensively lighted and ventilated, but they do keep heavy truck traffic from conflicting with the rest of the city's life.

Truck noise can be dealt with in a variety of ways. Air pollution from engine emissions is more difficult to control.

Automobile executives are quick to point out that automobiles make only a relatively small contribution to the most harmful pollutants in the atmosphere.

Clean emission standards for automobiles have been prescribed by law in the United States since 1973. The plan was that they were to be in effect by 1976. When the cars meet these standards, each automobile will emit 90 percent fewer air pollutants than had been emitted in 1970. The pollution caused by each automobile would be less than 5 percent of what it had been in 1963. This sounded fine; but the plan soon met with opposition.

A major role in reducing automobile emissions was to come from catalytic converters. These are containers of very small pellets of platinum and palladium that speed chemical reactions while remaining unchanged. Pellets are more effective than a block of material because they provide a larger surface area over which the exhaust gas can pass before being released.

Catalytic converters are effective at dealing with hydrocarbons and carbon monoxide. These are molecules containing hydrogen, carbon and oxygen. Poisonous carbon monoxide is converted with the addition of oxygen to harmless carbon dioxide. Nitrogen oxides are more difficult to catalyze.

Unfortunately there are costly side effects. A motor uses fuel less efficiently after the addition of an expensive and bulky catalytic converter. Lower mileage per gallon makes owners unhappy, particularly with sharply rising fuel costs.

To avoid wasting irreplaceable petroleum, manufacturers are experimenting with various other kinds of motors.

Safe and Sound

Before considering alternate motor systems, let us take a look at the efforts of manufacturers to counter complaints that their vehicles are not safe.

A number of experimental safety features have been developed. The aims are to protect occupants during head-on crashes, side impact, rear-end collisions, roll-overs, malfunction of brakes or other accidents. These are areas in which technical advances can be helpful.

Dealing with the criminal carelessness of drivers is more difficult. Too often people drive under the influence of alcohol or drugs or at speeds beyond the safety limits for the condition of the highway, their automobile, their own reaction time, or their state of health. Firm laws are needed to deal with these problems; but for laws to be effective, people must obey them. Each individual who drives must develop a sense of responsibility toward others on the road.

To return to the experimental safety features for cars, one area in which improvements are being attempted is the metal framework. Frames can be strengthened by the use of welded steel. But the total weight of the car has to be kept down within practical and economical limits. Lightweight construction can be combined with safety through honeycomb design. Door frames can be built of honeycomb material with countless small air spaces. This construction permits small units of the frame to "give" in case of a crash instead of a large unit buckling or snapping.

Fenders and hoods of flexible material that spring back into shape after contact are also being tried. Front and rear metal bumpers have been found to be almost useless during collision. At a speed as low as five miles per hour, most cars showed damage from impact, so bumpers are being enlarged and made more efficient. Some experimental cars have hydraulic bumpers that use water to give them flexibility. Others have extendable bumpers that reach out as much as 12 inches when the vehicle exceeds a speed of 25 or 30 mph.

Inside the passenger area, doors, pillers and dashboards are being padded with foam. Individual seat belts are being supplemented by other devices. One of the most promising safety devices is the air bag.

Air bags in compact containers are located on the instrument

A car designed for the future is the Tri-Vette, a fiberglass three-wheeled vehicle that registers up to 61 miles per gallon of gas. (Photo courtesy of Santa Barbara News-Press)

panel to protect the driver and front-seat passengers and on the back of the front seat for rear-seat passengers. They are connected to a sensor in the bumpers. If the car is sharply bumped, front or rear, the crash triggers the air bags. They balloon out to keep the passengers in place with gentle pressure. A fraction of a second later, they deflate to avoid interfering with the driver's performance.

One limitation of the air bag is evident in a chain-reaction crash involving a number of cars and more than one bump. The air bag has to be repacked in its container before it can respond to a second bump. So it does not protect passengers against a series of hard jolts.

Periscope rear-view mirrors and other helpful devices are also in production or in various stages of development. But there is a gap of several years between a research breakthrough and the actual marketing of a new device. Models must be constructed and thoroughly tested. Before the product can be put into production, cost-benefit analyses must be made. Tooling up for production is another time-consuming step. Even after a device is on the market there is no guarantee that the public will accept it. The reluctance of many people to use seat belts is one example of customer resistance to a valuable safety help.

Less Waste

The amount of petroleum fuel consumed by automobiles is a serious waste of energy. One study said that if oil continues to be used as a major fuel, the North American reserves will be badly depleted if not exhausted by the year 2000. Thirty years of heavy demand beyond the year 2000 would cut deeply into the remaining world reserves. By 1975, reliance on oil from the Middle East had seriously upset the economies of many countries.

Once the world's reserves of oil have all been pumped up from underground, they cannot be replaced. Formation of those oil pools took many millions of years. Petroleum is essential for many important and useful products such as plastics and synthetic rubber. We must look beyond our own lifetimes and save some of the limited supply for future generations.

Meanwhile, millions of automobiles continue to burn petroleum as if it were as abundant as sunlight. The average automobile in the United States in 1975 traveled about 13.5 miles on a gallon of gasoline. Those equipped with the early catalytic converters got even less mileage per gallon.

One manufacturer of small cars referred to large, fuel-extravagant cars as "dinosaurs" doomed to vanish like the prehistoric creatures. Since a one-ton car generally gets twice the mileage of a two-ton car, good sense would seem to dictate using small cars to save fuel.

By the early 1970s in the Los Angeles area more than half the cars sold were the small "compacts." The trend soon spread across the country. In most European and Asian countries the ratio has long been considerably higher.

Japan, for example, has for some years had a very high sales tax on large cars. This tax was planned to keep American cars out of the Japanese market. It has also succeeded in keeping the cars on Japan's crowded streets small.

States such as California made a start in the direction of encouraging the use of small cars by charging higher annual registration fees for expensive cars. But these fees were not set high enough to discourage anyone who could afford to buy a large car. The California fee is not related to size or gas consumption; it is based on the car's market value. After a few years the fee for a big, old, gas-hungry car with a low resale value is quite small.

Other methods for cutting down fuel consumption have been considered. Some of these are high sales taxes and registration fees geared to fuel use; high taxes on gasoline itself; the rationing of gasoline; and the prohibition of nonessential Sunday driving. But most people do not really understand the long-range seriousness of the limited petroleum reserves. They do not feel that it is necessary for them to give up the pleasure and convenience of using their cars as they wish.

Another alternative to the problem of petroleum-devouring cars is to develop a substitute fuel.

New Fuels

There is one simple and satisfactory substitute for petroleum fuel. This is natural gas. It works effectively in automobile motors, and the wastes it leaves as it burns are much less polluting than those of gasoline.

The main obstacle is that an owner of a present-day automobile needs a kit to convert a motor to use natural gas. Even if the car has been converted, the new fuel may be hard to find because it is in great demand by industries and is already in rather short supply.

Why suggest it, then? Well, natural gas is a term used for several compounds of hydrogen and carbon that are known as hydrocarbons. Propane, butane, ethane and methane are some of the better-known natural gases. These various compounds are often separated for various uses. Natural gas is found with petroleum deposits. Methane is found in coal mines, where it can be very dangerous. The future of methane as an alternative fuel lies in the fact that it is formed by decaying plant and animal matter—and that is plentiful.

Usable methane can be produced from sewage, for example. Disposal of sewage and other solid wastes is a major problem for cities today. Some plants are already in use to convert these wastes to methane gas. Wider use of this conversion process could solve a basic urban management problem and provide an additional fuel stock as well.

A scattered few thousand motorists have purchased an English invention known as the "autogas convert device" which uses homemade methane in automobiles.

The basic ingredient in the home production of the methane fuel is a pile of barnyard manure. About 100 pounds of manure will produce a tankful of gas. Straw and water are added to the pile. The straw provides the carbon, the water supplies hydrogen. After about two smelly weeks, a batch of colorless, odorless methane gas (CH_4) results. While not everyone will want a manure pile "cooking" in the backyard, commercial production of methane gas from plentiful animal and human wastes is quite practicable.

There are other possibilities for alternate fuels. Gas from coal was used during World War II to run some cars and buses, particularly in England. Huge bags filled with gas were strapped to the roofs of those vehicles. More convenient ways to handle the fuel could be developed. And new processes for turning coal to gas are gaining in importance. There is much, much more coal underground to be mined than there is liquid petroleum to be pumped up the world around. But mining scars the land, and coal is not available in unlimited supplies either.

Hydrogen gas can, with some adjustments, also be used in a standard engine when combined with a small quantity of oxygen. Some cars using hydrogen are already on the road. Its use as fuel eliminates crankcase explosions and knock, so an engine runs quietly. It is efficient, releasing large amounts of energy when it is burned. And it leaves no fumes or solid pollutants—only water vapor. Hydrogen gas can also be produced from plain water by running an electric current through it, a process called electrolysis.

New Motors

Many new fuels require changes in the design of motors. Beyond this, there is the possibility of a radical change in the basic principle of automobile motors. One design that has aroused widespread interest is the rotary engine.

Named the Wankel for its German inventor, the rotary engine was perfected in Japan years ago, but it is fairly new to the mass automobile market.

To appreciate the advantages of the rotary engine, it will help to take a brief look at the traditional internal-combustion engine. It has cylinders shaped like tubes, with a one-way opening at the top controlled by a valve. Gasoline, mixed to fine mist in the carburetor

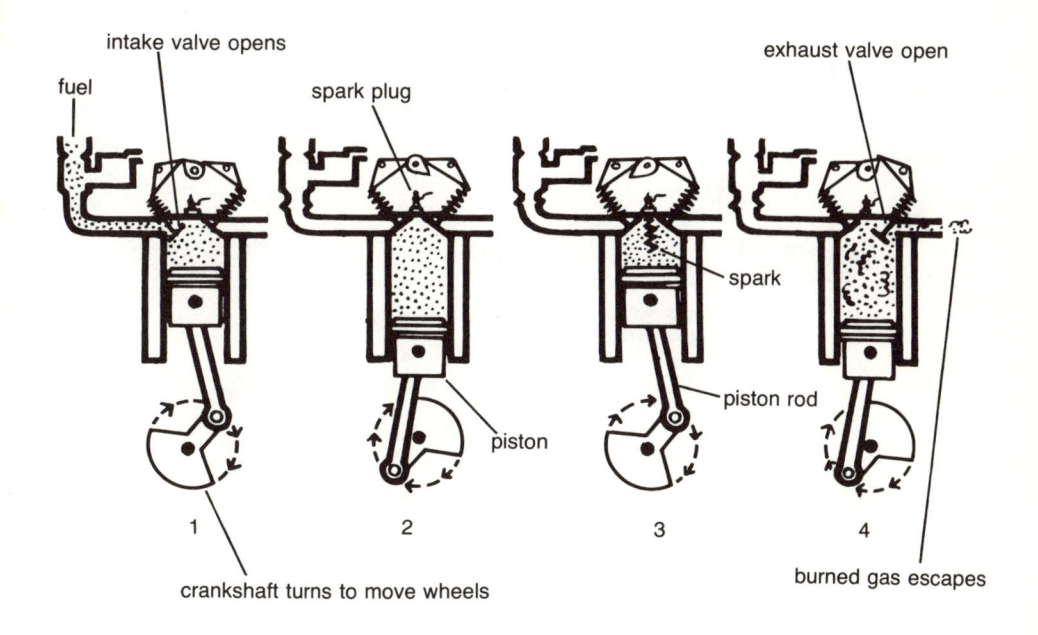

1) Fuel enters the cylinder, piston goes down; 2) piston goes up, compresses fuel; 3) spark ignites a fuel explosion, pushes piston down; 4) piston starts up, pushes out burned gas.

with the addition of air, enters the cylinder through the valve. A plunger called the piston moves up from the bottom of the cylinder to compress the fuel. When it is compressed, a spark from the spark plug jumps across it and causes it to explode. The force of the explosion forces the piston down and it turns the crankshaft which moves the wheels.

The rotary engine is simpler. It has an oval motor unit. Fresh air is sucked in and mixed with the fuel as in the internal-combustion engine. Instead of a piston, it has a triangular centerpiece that rotates. This rotation results in the repeated reduction of the size of the chamber where the air and fuel mixture is located. When the mixture is most compressed, a spark ignites it. The fuel explodes, and the expansion of this explosion pushes the rotor around farther, also driving the shaft. The residue from the exploded fuel is then forced out through an outlet.

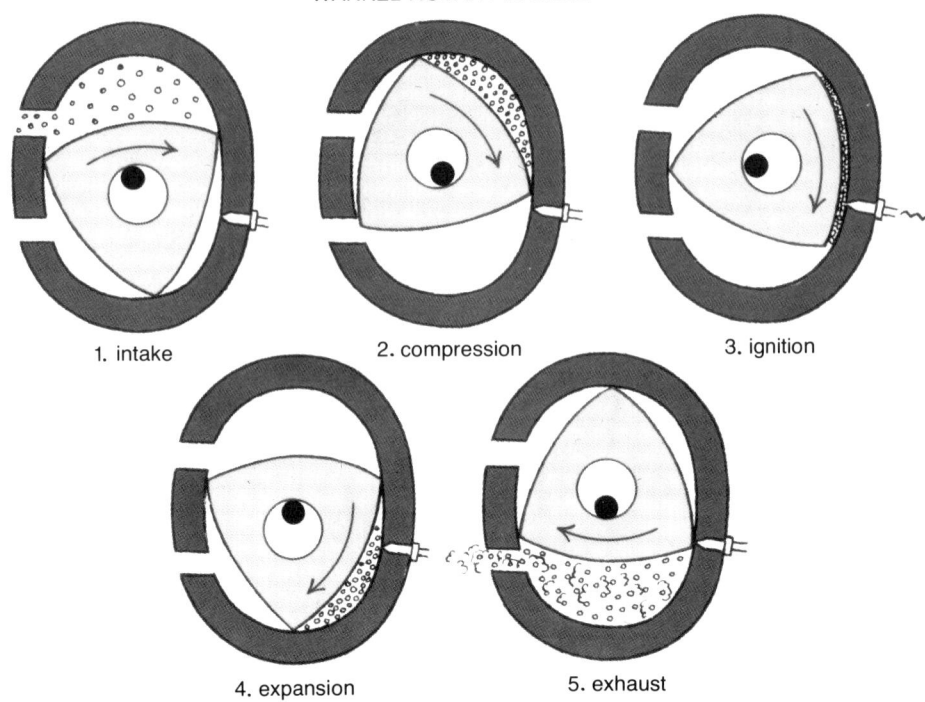

WANKEL ROTARY ENGINE

1. intake   2. compression   3. ignition

4. expansion   5. exhaust

A mixture of air and gasoline is drawn into the firing chamber of the Wankel engine, then compressed, ignited and expelled. It has fewer moving parts than the standard internal combustion engine.

The Wankel engine is small and light. It occupies so little space that the car hood can be lower, which gives the driver better visibility than in many larger cars. There are fewer parts because pistons and valves have been eliminated, so both manufacturing and maintenance costs are reduced.

Inexpensive, low-octane fuel works well in the Wankel motor. Waste gasoline that leaks out is burned in a thermal reactor outside the motor. The burning oxidizes the carbon monoxide, changing poisonous CO to harmless CO_2. Unburned hydrocarbons and carbon monoxide, which cause most of the pollution from automobiles, are cut by 97 to 98 percent. Nitrogen oxides are also much reduced because the peak operating heat is lower. But this lower temperature has the negative result of cutting the engine's fuel efficiency (or miles per gallon). Engineers are working to improve this.

Wankels have been in use in boats, snowmobiles and model airplanes for years. Delays in their general use in automobiles have been caused by several factors. One has been the huge cost involved in converting manufacturing plants to their production and adapting automobile body styles. Another factor has been the need for improvement of their efficiency in the use of fuel.

Another new clean, efficient and very promising engine is the Honda stratified-charge engine developed in Japan. It meets the United States' 1976 clean-engine requirements without a catalytic converter and offers almost 30 miles per gallon of gas. The secret of its success is a pre-combustion chamber with a spark plug in the cylinder head. Some fuel burns there before moving into the cylinder where the combustion is controlled. It starts with a rich fuel-air mix that is easy to ignite, but it is diluted to a lighter mixture that is more efficient in using all the hydrocarbons and is very clean-burning.

The limitations of early electric cars are being overcome by technical advances that increase the range and speed of the vehicles. (Photo courtesy of B & Z Electric Car)

Charge It

There is one power source that does not pollute the air above and around the highways at all. This is electricity. It is enjoying a comeback after decades of neglect in the transportation field.

Electric taxi service was introduced in New York City in 1898, and private electric cars were available at about the same time. In the early days of the automobile, small elegant electric cars with a graceful steering bar instead of a wheel were popular. They were considered especially suitable for lady drivers because piston engines in those days had to be started with muscle-straining cranking.

The electric cars had limitations. They were not very speedy. They were not suitable for long highway journeys because of the need for frequent recharging. Each recharging took several hours.

When self-starters eliminated the need for cranking gasoline-fueled cars, the electrics lost their largest advantage. As the "gas buggies" grew in size, speed and power, electric cars could no longer compete. During the 1920s these small, silent cars vanished from city streets. For many years they were represented only by the very small three-wheeled models planned for handicapped people. There were also electric off-the-street vehicles such as golf carts.

During the 1970s the electric-powered automobile seems about to stage a major comeback. The big manufacturers are still devoting their attention largely to internal-combustion engines. But many new manufacturers have entered the field with various electric-powered vehicles.

The weaknesses and limitations of early electric cars are being overcome by recent technical advances. Their speed has increased to become competitive once again. Until the 1920s first electric and then steam-powered cars held the world speed records.

The driving range possible between battery charges has increased too. By the mid-1970s a battery charge could take an electric car about 50 miles or 70 kilometers. Most average American cars are driven 27 miles or 44 kilometers per day, so a 50-mile range seems adequate. Recharging time is down to 30 minutes.

A real research breakthrough has been achieved involving the use of a flywheel. Flywheels have been around for many centuries. When you spin a top or wind the spring of a child's toy, you are using the principle of the flywheel to store energy

FLYWHEEL IN HYBRID VEHICLE

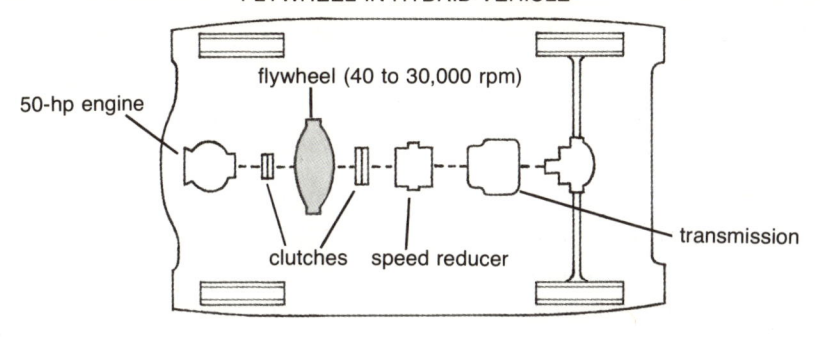

flywheel (40 to 30,000 rpm)

50-hp engine

clutches   speed reducer

transmission

EVOLUTION OF THE SUPER FLYWHEEL

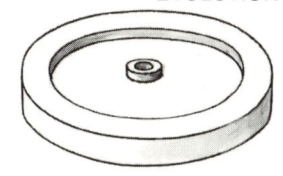

1. Rim flywheel. Most widely used type.

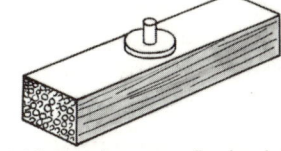

4. Music-wire super flywheel. Can be spun at ultra-high speeds.

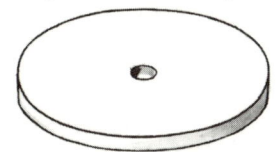

2. Solid steel disk. Can be spun faster to store more energy.

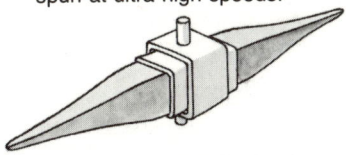

5. Tapered bar super flywheel.

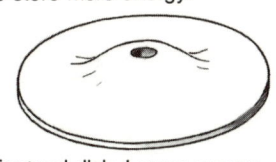

3. Tapered disk. Larger energy storage capacity.

6. Double-wedge super flywheel. Reduced drag because of bonded filaments.

Researchers found that electric cars drained their batteries quickly when they were accelerating to start up or to pass another car. But not much power was needed for normal driving. A system has been developed to store up extra energy in the flywheel when a car is using less than maximum power. The flywheel rotates on a vertical axis. When acceleration is needed, extra power comes from the flywheel. The motor can run at a smooth level, conserving the battery charge. Some of the heat energy generated by applying the brakes can also be stored in the flywheel. In 1950 the Swiss built a small car that traveled one kilometer just on the energy stored in the flywheel, without a battery in the car. The flywheel can be recharged in two minutes from any suitably equipped utility pole.

By 1960 this idea was applied to buses in the San Francisco area. They could travel free of power lines for up to six miles, serving the side streets in any area. Then they returned to trolley cables for recharging.

For a small half-ton city runabout or a small boat or a piece of garden equipment, it is now possible to plug into a standard electric outlet overnight to spin a 220-pound flywheel until it is tightly wound. In the morning all that is needed is to unplug the machine, throw the switch and drive off for up to 100 miles (160 km).

A super flywheel that will take higher speeds of rotation and produce more drive energy can be made of fine music wires or of fibers clamped together for strength greater than steel. Its applications have not yet been fully explored.

Electricity is not really free power. Most of it is produced by the burning of some fuel in a steam or nuclear power plant. Only hydroelectric plants operate without depleting fuel reserves, because they use only water power, and the water cycle is powered by the sun. Within a few years solar heat collectors should also be running some electric generators. One experimental electric automobile uses very cold liquid hydrogen to feed fuel cells that provide electricity to run the car. Hydrogen is almost as plentiful as sunshine.

Matching Power to Use

No single fuel or power source will answer all needs in the wide and varied field of motorized transport. Gas turbines, in which a turbine wheel is substituted for pistons in cylinders, may be used to power heavy-duty trucks and buses. Hydrogen, methane or perhaps low-emission diesel fuel will be used in many passenger cars for long-distance travel. And electricity will probably power vans for local deliveries and small cars for errands around town.

In making forecasts one must always leave room for the wholly new and unexpected development. Remember that before the 1950s there were no jet liners, no supersonic planes and no spaceships. The major advancements that tomorrow may bring for automobiles remain to be seen.

Sharing

Even working with the materials we have today considerable improvements can be made. One quick way to economize in the reuse of scarce fuels is simply to increase the number of passengers per trip. For commuting trips of about ten miles, car pools provide the most convenient and economical transportation.

About the most expensive transportation, on the other hand, is the one-driver/passenger car, so commuters are being encouraged to join forces. Businesses often offer preferred parking spaces to cars used for pools. Freeways may open special high-speed, one-way lanes now used by express buses to well-filled passenger cars.

Many businesses, schools and local radio stations have set up grid maps of their local areas. Commuters supply their home locations, places of work and hours of work. Then computers match up drivers with riders. The computer then provides lists of possible poolers.

Within a two-month period one big-city radio station received more than 500,000 applications in response to its offer of a pooling service. Each driver was sent a list of ten potential passengers. The aim was to have at least three people in each car. Each such pool removes two cars from the roads, with all of their polluting side effects. It also saves their fuel.

More informal neighborhood pools for shopping and other errands do not need the services of a computer. Higher parking and toll road or bridge charges and special credits for car pools encourage this kind of sharing.

After some experience with the car-pool plan, many poolers agree that shared commuting is not only cheaper and cleaner but is more companionable and pleasanter.

Motorcycles

Motorcycles, two-wheeled and gasoline-powered, are very popular for sport and recreation. Because they are small, swift and maneuverable, motorcycles are widely used by law-enforcement officers. They also appeal to young people. Motorcycles are not as expensive as automobiles, gasoline consumption is much lower and the rider has a great sense of personal power and freedom.

One passenger can usually be seated directly behind the driver.

One-wheeled sidecars to hold additional passengers are available but are not as popular as they once were. Some three-wheeled models have been developed especially for use by handicapped persons. Motorcycles do have a place in the world of daily transportation, but there are serious drawbacks.

Motorcycles travel at high speed but offer their riders almost no protection from weather or, more important, from serious injury in case of accident. Used for off-road recreation, they have helped destroy beaches, deserts and other open lands where they have been carelessly driven. The high level of noise produced is also a serious charge against wider use of motorcycles.

Pedal Power

Private and convenient transportation need not depend on either electricity, petroleum products or natural gas for fuel. Food can be the fuel for leg muscles that is converted to the energy to move pedals. The bicycle is the most popular pedal-power vehicle. It has been widely used for transportation in countries where distances are short and the land is level. Denmark and the Netherlands are examples of bicycle countries. Bicycles are the leading form of privately owned transport in some countries such as India because the purchase price and cost for upkeep are low. Even in the United States they are regaining much of the popularity they enjoyed before the upsurge of the automobile.

Where bicycles travel the same roads as much heavier and speedier automobiles, safety is an important factor. Separate bicycle routes or lanes are being laid out in many communities for those who commute or do errands by bicycle. This is most practical where the distances involved are not much more than five miles.

Another important factor in many areas is protection from the weather. Providing adequate cover for the rider necessitates a larger frame than that of a bicycle. To fill this need, a pedal-powered car on a four-wheel base has been developed. This pedicar has a transmission that offers five speeds and a reverse gear. It can be pedaled along at about 12 mph (20 km/h) when the driver pedals as if he were walking briskly on a generally level road. Using as much energy as for jogging can bring the speed up to about 18 mph or 30 km/h.

These experimental pedal-mobiles are patterned after small automobiles, just as the earliest automobiles were patterned after horse-drawn buggies—even to buggy whips on the dashboards! The pedal-mobiles have an adjustable, high-backed driver's seat in an enclosed cab with a hatch back for easy handling of bulky parcels. They offer safety features such as disc brakes, rear-view mirror and headlights.

Man- or woman-powered vehicles of this sort produce no air or noise pollution. They use no scarce fuels. Human energy requires only food and water for fuel plus frequent rest stops to "recharge batteries." The exercise is good for the driver, too. There is a definite place for pedal power in the balanced, multimodal transportation system that will be needed in our world tomorrow.

Even bicycle traffic and parking need control, as shown by this patrolled bike parking lot in Nanking, People's Republic of China.

MOVING PEOPLE: A BALANCED SYSTEM

"Look at any major metropolitan freeway system at the end of a business day," a transportation engineer suggests. "Three things will immediately be clear. First, traffic moves at a pace far below the speed for which the freeway was designed. Second, most of the cars carry only one person, the driver; they are being used at a level far below that for which they were designed. Third, a pall of noxious fumes hangs over the whole area. It's not the kind of air for which human lungs were designed. There has to be a better way to move people."

Numerous governmental groups, as well as countless private citizens, agree. Their concern has spurred many studies since the late 1950s. The goal of these studies is a new system of travel and transport that will be fast, safe, convenient, comfortable, quiet and pollution-free.

A Range of Needs

No one kind of transportation, however new and revolutionary it may be, can fill all of today's needs. We need a range of many kinds of services, with each supplementing and complementing the others.

These are the basic kinds of services that are required:

1. Airplanes and a good network of railways for long-distance and cross-country travel. Locomotives will pull trains of cars along the railways, and some of these railway cars will be designed to carry family automobiles.

2. Fast, light turbine-powered railway trains for shorter runs between cities.

3. Commuter lines with self-powered cars rather than heavy locomotives running between suburbs and central cities.

4. Small "people movers" vehicles that move on traffic-free guided routes. These will service "point-to-point" routes, connecting, for example, an airport or a suburban university campus with the downtown area.

5. Underground railways or subways, surface-level and elevated mass-transit systems within large cities. These systems will include self-powered cars, trackless trolleys and buses.

6. Personal rapid-transit service within central-city areas, using small semiprivate "pods" that operate on traffic-free guided routes and offer many of the advantages of private cars or taxis.

Who Will Use Them?

Surely such a long list of options should satisfy all possible needs and desires! So it would seem at first glance. But most people who have been used to the comfort and privacy and the door-to-door service of a private car will not be satisfied with service that herds them into a small space with a lot of other people, after waiting impatiently for it to arrive. If the vehicle then stops and starts along the way and finally does not take them exactly where they want to go, they probably won't use it!

In the early 1970s about 90 percent of all trips in the United States were made by car. If that percentage is to be cut it is important that any new projects that are developed attract and satisfy automobile users. But even in the United States there are many people who do not travel by automobile.

In 1972, 21 percent of all families in the United States did not own an automobile. Half of the families whose head was over sixty-five years of age had no car. Less than half the families classified as poor owned a car, and they desperately needed public transportation to get quickly and cheaply to their jobs.

In crowded inner cities, owning a car was—and still is—simply not practical. Only about 14 percent of inner-city families had them in 1972.

By 1970 it was extremely difficult for many people to reach work without an automobile. In many areas, even day-to-day errands and shopping were nearly impossible for those who did not drive.

Many public transportation systems let their facilities fall into sad states of disrepair as private cars took over. The right-of-ways for vehicles that ran on tracks had been abandoned. Services such as home delivery of baked goods, fresh vegetables and fruits, groceries and other goods had been cut back or stopped.

Now with a move under way to lessen people's dependence on automobiles, it is clear than new transportation systems are badly needed. Many cities have set up studies to determine how most of the needs of people can be met in the best possible way. Let us see how one of these studies proceeds.

To Start a Study

It takes money to start a study. The money usually is appropriated by the city council. Then the council retains a consulting firm of experts to study the city as an economic system.

"We have to understand the community as a whole," one transportation engineer with a consulting firm points out, "before we can even think of planning a new urban transportation system for it."

Transportation cannot be dealt with by itself. It is interwoven with countless other elements of modern life. So the "economic system analysis" of the city involves not only engineers but economists, mathematicians, urban planners and government officials as well as business people of the city.

They consider many kinds of intertwined problems. Power resources, air pollution, different possible uses of the available land, and the aesthetic quality—the beauty and attractiveness—of the city as a whole are a few of the topics considered.

Analysts tabulate all the city's businesses and industries. It is important to know what raw materials are imported, what products are shipped out, how many people are employed and where and at what hours these employees work. Raw materials, finished products and working people all rely on transportation. The analysts also study the city's residential facilities. And they take a close look at the present transportation system, including private cars, buses, subways and whatever else the city may offer.

Construction on the first section of the $6 billion subway system in our nation's capital was completed in 1976. (Photo courtesy of the Washington Metropolitan Transit Authority)

These researchers gather their information from many sources. The Chamber of Commerce can tell them about local businesses; tax records can provide information too. City plans tell them about streets, tracks, available land and zoning restrictions. Door-to-door surveys indicate what householders need and want in the way of transportation. When all the information is compiled, the analysts put together their economic model of the city, using slide rules and computers to bring all their figures together into orderly patterns.

Now it is time to have more meetings. The team expands to include specialists in different power or propulsion systems, in electrical problems, industrial design, style and color and many other fields. These experts pool all their ideas. They find that the wide-ranging discussions they call "brainstorming" often spark ideas that might not have occurred to one person working alone.

The analysts generally find that these are the principal problems facing the present public transportation system:

1. Not enough service to non-drivers who need to reach jobs or shops and services.

2. Limited routes, mainly along rail lines (for subways or inter-urban trains).

3. Uneven schedules, with little or no service during some hours, for people who work odd shifts.

4. The discomfort of waiting on platforms or corners unprotected from the weather.

5. Being crowded into vehicles with uncomfortable seats or standing room only.

6. The difficulty of boarding the vehicles for the aged, handicapped and those who have to carry parcels and luggage.

7. The slowness of travel, with many stops along the way.

The drivers of private cars have their own list of complaints. Congestion on travel routes and the hazards of driving in traffic top these lists. Many people also are concerned about the amount of land that highways take out of more productive use. Highways cutting through cities lessen the value of the nearby property too.

The experts evaluate all the points people have brought up for consideration. The features that people value most in transportation of any kind are:

1. Protection from weather and other hazards at the pickup site.

2. Adequate seating.

3. Privacy.

4. Short waiting time for service.

5. No delays en route, and no transfers.

6. Assurance of arriving safely and at the planned time.

The planners begin to work on ideas to meet all those needs. To eliminate all the present problems and to provide all the things people want sounds like a difficult task. But the systems planners have other responsibilities such as computing costs too.

To analyze the number of people and the amount of goods that the new system must transport daily is relatively easy. They know the length of the trips people take, where they go to and from, at what times they travel and other statistics. They study the way other cities have solved similar problems and consider all the possibilities for combining different kinds of services for both long and short trips. Adding imaginative touches for improving services that have been tried elsewhere is often exciting and stimulating. But there is a lot of plain hard work.

More or less detailed specifications for all the proposed equipment have to be drawn up before the costs can be estimated. This is an extremely important part of the study because the costs for any new public transportation system are bound to be very high.

The experts have to consider the financial feasibility of their plans. Will the system be profitable for private investment or will it require a government subsidy?

The answer to this in almost every instance is that a subsidy (monetary help) will be needed. On a plain dollar basis a new transport system is necessarily more costly than the fares paid by riders can support. It should, however, provide enough other benefits to the community to make the use of public money worthwhile.

In San Francisco's Bay Area Rapid Transit system, for example, for every five cents paid in fare in 1975, an additional ten cents had to come from taxes. In return for their very large public contribution to the system, the people hoped to get a reduction in air and noise pollution from less road traffic and a reduction of the vibrations that weakened nearby buildings. They also hoped for safer travel to work with thousands of people freed from driving in congested traffic. They hoped to save additional land from being swallowed up by highways and parking lots, so that the whole area might be more attractive in the future.

The indirect benefits have to be added to the direct benefits to users in the form of rides and goods carried. Only when all the benefits for years ahead are estimated can the experts make the cost-benefit equation balance.

The first stage of the systems analysis usually takes about nine months to complete. When it is in hand, the experts have a clear idea of the average speed the new transportation system should provide, the distance between stations that would offer convenient service and the size of vehicles that might be most economical. They know what travel presently costs the people of the city, so they can compare these current costs with a range of possible fare rates on the new system. Soon they are ready to move into the second stage.

The next step is the design of the actual units for the new project.

Specifications have to be exact so that manufacturers can bid to supply elements for the system. Tracks or guide rails, cars or cabs, stations or power systems all must be planned in complete detail.

Scale models and mock-ups of parts of the system are constructed. And the manufacturers' engineers put their slide rules and computers to work on cost analyses and bids.

When bids are in and contracts have been let, the manufacturers build samples called prototypes for testing. This second stage, the design and construction of the prototypes, usually takes about a year and a half.

Then comes stage three for which the public has been waiting. The equipment is installed and put into operation. The public can then judge how well the new project really works.

Fares in the Box

Engineers can calculate the costs and plan the construction of the equipment. They can estimate how long the equipment will last, what depreciation there will be over the years, and even how many accidents will probably occur on the lines in spite of every precaution. They can estimate how many passengers will use the service and what the fares should be. But they cannot tell how well the public will accept and use a new and somewhat unfamiliar system.

The amount charged as fare can influence the success of the project. But this is not as important as one might think. Manning ticket-sales booths, installing fare boxes or turnstiles or hiring workers to collect fares are expensive. Some cities have found that as much as 50 percent of public transportation operating costs goes into the collection of fares.

A city may decide to make all public transportation free. Rome offered free bus rides in an effort to get cars off the streets. Other cities have set a low flat fare for any ride within the system.

Even offering rides free will not necessarily make a new system popular, though. It must work well technically, though there are almost certainly a few hitches at the start. It must work well with the old bus lines or whatever has been in use. It must be comfortable and convenient for its users and have a desirable effect on the life of the community. If it accomplishes all these things over a period of time, it will be worth the trouble.

The rapid-transit systems in Washington, D.C., and San Francisco are the first new ones to be built in the United States in over 50 years. (Photo courtesy of Rohr Industries)

One of the most promising of the new kinds of service being developed for large cities as a result of studies like this is the Personal Rapid Transit, known as the PRT.

Personal Rapid Transit

Personal Rapid Transit systems are planned principally for central-city use.

Most cities above 200,000 in population have rather compact central "downtown" areas. Many business firms maintain offices there. Generally traffic is very congested, and parking is difficult and expensive. Buses and subways are jammed at peak hours, and they never can offer routes that are flexible enough to take all of the people exactly where they want to go.

Mini-bus routes have been established in some central cities to serve these crowded business areas. They have proved helpful but are not complete solutions to the problem. Something entirely new is needed. As we saw before, the development of a new project must start with a survey.

The study centers first on a map of the business section, keyed to show where the most people are employed. On this map a grid of routes is worked out that will take any rider within a block or two of any destination in that area. The routes must be definite because the experts must plan fixed guideways for the PRT. Small cabs, powered by electricity, travel along these routes.

To be effective, these guideways for the PRT will have to link up with other public transportation outside the central district. There will be stations at entrances to express highways. Commuters from the suburbs can park their cars or change from express buses to the PRT. Guideways will also run into railway terminals for the convenience of travelers who reach the central city by train.

A central PRT grid of one-way guidetracks with short side "spur" tracks that lead to small PRT stations is included in initial plans. The stations are to be located inside business buildings, department stores and the like to offer passengers protection from the weather.

The guideways and the stations are raised a floor or two above street level to avoid street traffic. Planners picture not only the PRT guideways but other pedestrian bridges linking downtown buildings above the street level. With automobile traffic practically eliminated from this section, the once noisy, traffic-crowded streets can become attractive, pollution-free garden walkways.

The bus is likely to be the mainstay of transit systems in the United States for years to come. This sleekly designed vehicle incorporates recent technological advancements. (Photo courtesy of General Motors)

When you are ready to leave one of these garden spots for a ride on the PRT, you stroll to the nearest station. Probably there is one in the store where you have been shopping or in the building where you work. Signs guide you there. You drop your fare into a slot or perhaps slip a credit card into another slot. Then a door opens to let you step into the waiting area.

The waiting area is not very large because almost no one is kept waiting long here. Even at peak hours there is rarely a wait of more than a minute for one of the 3,000 cabs that serve this route.

Chances are that there is a cab waiting for you, with its battery or motor being charged as it stands. The whole front and top of the small cab swing up and back as a unit, like a giant clam shell opening. This doorway about six feet high by five feet wide (or nearly two by one and a half meters) permits riders to step in without climbing or stooping. Wheelchairs, perambulators or heavy bundles can be taken into these cabs without difficulty.

In the cab, which may have room for four or six passengers, you take a seat, press a button on a lighted map to indicate where you want to go, and the door closes gently. The cab moves slowly and smoothly along the station spur to the main line. There it slides into the flow of traffic without a pause because the speed of all the cabs is regulated from a central computer.

While this system is being perfected, the cabs move at an average speed of about 30 mph or 50 km/h, about six seconds' travel time apart. A single lane can handle about 2,000 vehicles an hour. This speed and distance allow a generous safety margin in case of any sudden stops. Engineers feel that speeds of up to 120 mph or 200 km/h will be possible eventually and that cabs will be able to travel safely spaced just one second's travel time apart.

A journey anywhere on this line will not take more than a few minutes. But if you should change your mind about where you want to get off, you can press another button to notify the computer center of the change.

As your cab approaches your destination, the cab will move onto another low-speed station spur. When it reaches the passenger loading platform there, the car will be pulled sideways by a retractable platform. It will rest on skids with its floor flush with the platform. This will make your disembarking easy, whether you and the other passengers are on foot, crutches or in wheelchairs.

While the cab is off the guide rail, an electromagnet at the edge of the platform holds the cab steady. A power rail below keeps the electrical equipment working so that lights, heating, cooling and communication devices are always ready.

These cabs offer nearly as much privacy as an automobile, though at peak hours passengers will probably have to share cabs, at least in the early PRT systems. The cabs will be fully as comfortable as automobiles, with the added advantage of offering a relaxing ride, complete with background music, instead of the strain and responsibility of driving with the problem of parking at the end of the drive.

Some PRT systems may have standard cab shapes fitted together to form larger units more like buses or full-length trains. But they will be fully as comfortable as the small ones, if less private.

Optimistic planners think that by 1990 these services will be expanding to the suburbs. Somewhat similar services called "people movers" are already in service at a few airports.

Special-Purpose People Pods

Some of these suburban-link people movers are designed to hang beneath overhead guideways. They may share right-of-ways with utility power lines, since in the suburbs there will not be close-built, multistoried buildings to support the guideways. Others are designed to operate over guideways shaped like long shallow concrete troughs. The "people pods" may have wheels or be supported on air cushions. They may be propelled by electric "third rails" or by linear induction motors.

Some cabs are the size of buses, holding as many as forty passengers. They will be quite comfortable, even if you should have to stand, for the trip will be short, speedy and smooth.

The smaller cabs, sometimes called Multimodal Capsules, really represent an extension of the PRTs. Designers hope that as the systems grow, cabs or capsules can be switched from one line to another.

These very small "people pods" promise to be economical to build, using a great deal of available automobile manufacturing equipment, and will be economical to operate. They are planned to be very flexible. They can be transported on railway cars, twenty pods to a car. They can travel on special flatbed trucks, ten pods to a

The monocab system consists of six-passenger vehicles that are suspended from an elevated guideway and a computer center that dispatches vehicles to all passenger pick-up areas. (Photo courtesy of Rohr Industries)

truck body. Or they can move independently over shorter distances on their own set of guideways.

If future plans work out, the cab or pod will be able to move up to the loading level or down to the ground level of the airport on an escalatorlike conveyor, as well as horizontally down long corridors. This will eliminate the long walks and flights of stairs or escalators that have been inconvenient for many passengers at many airports.

Since privacy in travel appears high on many people's lists, the small size of these pods is an important advantage. At an airport, for example, a passenger can arrange to wait, if he wishes, in the privacy of his small compartment until his plane is called.

The flexibility, relative economy and privacy offered by the people pods seem certain to make them very popular, once they are widely installed.

Larger people movers are planned to carry big groups of people along fixed guideways, to and from airport and other special destinations. They will be simply one element in a complex system. At their terminals most passengers will transfer to their own waiting automobiles or to airlines, railways or buses.

Express Buses

Buses must avoid traffic delays if they are to persuade workers to leave cars at home and ride the bus. Special high-speed lanes reserved for buses provide a relatively simple solution and are already in use on some expressways.

On express lanes, buses and, in some cases, car-pool automobiles with four or more passengers can travel between 50 and 70 mph (or 80 to 110 km/h) if the higher speeds are legal. They leave the express lane only as they approach a terminal or other stop where they take on or discharge passengers.

These express lanes have been very successful. In the vicinity of Washington, D.C., bus travel to the city increased 300 percent during the first three years of express service. Here, as in some other places, the express lanes reverse direction: They carry buses toward the city in the morning and back to the suburbs at day's end. Travel by express bus is cheaper and faster than driving and parking a car. It also offers bonuses in convenience, comfort and sociability.

Commuters from at least one satellite community near Washington have formed social clubs on their regular buses. They serve refreshments during the pleasant rides to and from work. Other commuters enjoy using the travel time for reading.

Automated Highways

A little farther ahead in the world of tomorrow is the automated highway. It will replace some of today's express highways, or at least certain lanes on them. Eventually this will be available for transcontinental travel.

A control unit on each automobile will be provided that will permit you to travel the automated routes. This is how it will work: As you drive up the access ramp at an entry point, you push a button on a map or sign to indicate your destination. And you pay the amount indicated for that distance. Equipment at the entry point checks that your car is properly equipped. If it is not, your fare is returned and you will not be able to enter.

If all is well, another automatic checker notes the point at which you wish to leave the highway. Even though your car is properly equipped, you will not be allowed to enter the automated stretch unless there is going to be space for you to exit smoothly when you reach your chosen exit point. There will be no traffic slow-ups on this highway!

Once the exit has been affirmatively checked, your car is hooked electronically onto a buried cable and fed smoothly into the moving stream of traffic. Because the traffic does not have to rely on the reaction time of human drivers who make errors, cars can safely travel closer together and at higher speed than on ordinary highways. The automated section of highway can thus accommodate many more cars per hour than if they were manually controlled. And the drivers will reach the end of the automated stretch of their journey rested and fresh.

Buses will have to be adapted for use on the automated highways too. On automated stretches they will not need drivers, so the bus may be in the form of a trailer with a detachable cab. The cab will be detached as the bus enters the automated highway. And another driver will wait at the exit in another trailer cab to be hooked onto the bus body. These are known as dual-mode buses.

Bus at Your Call

Sometimes there is simply not a bus route close enough to provide convenient service. Let us say that a grandmother who does not have a car has been babysitting with her grandchildren. Now it is time for her to start home, but it is not easy for her daughter to drive her, with dinner time drawing near—and there is not a convenient bus route. Fortunately their community has Dial-a-Bus service.

Grandmother telephones. In some communities she would walk to a nearby corner and drop a coin into a telephone slot and receive a ticket. At the same time, a signal in the bus-company office indicates the location from which the call or signal has come. The computer dispatcher adds this call-box location—or telephoned address—to its list of pick-up points. The nearest bus is directed to pick up the passenger.

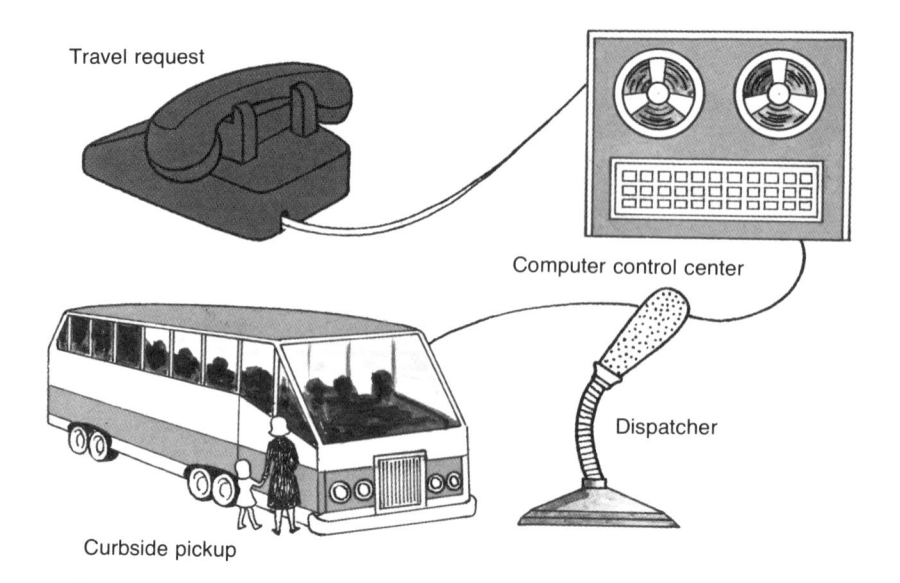

Travel request

Computer control center

Dispatcher

Curbside pickup

Grandmother steps into a small, low-slung bus and rides to her destination. Or she may be taken to a central terminal in a shopping center, where she will transfer to a bus headed for her neighborhood. This bus will take her to her door.

This service is not revolutionary. The mini-buses are familiar-looking. The service offers a much needed, less expensive extension of taxicab service, especially in small communities. These buses also act as feeder lines to carry passengers to long-distance buses, PRT systems or railway trains. The problem in some communities is how to finance this valuable service until its economic basis is sound.

Token-in-the-Slot

Another personalized service providing public transportation between that of a taxi and a rental car is being tried in a number of European cities. It is based on small two-seated electric cars. These are lined up at "electric taxi stands" scattered around the city. Whenever a car is not in use, it is plugged in at a taxi stand for recharging. Much of this recharging is done at night, when the use of electricity is low, so the cars do not burden the local power plants.

When a customer comes along, he checks the waiting cars at a stand, looking for one with a charged battery. A small green light might indicate this. The customer then unplugs the car and puts a token into a slot to activate the vehicle.

For each unit of distance driven—perhaps a half mile—another token is inserted to keep the car in motion. By this simple means the customer can drive anywhere in town, so long as the journey ends at another stand where the car can be plugged in again.

Any one of a variety of systems for handling the tokens can be used. There has to be a charge for them, of course. But there must also be some means of identifying the customer in case a car is not properly returned to a plug-in outlet. Each token may carry the license number of the customer or it may have a serial number that was recorded when the customer purchased it.

For non-drivers, some of these small cars can be available with drivers on a taxi-hire basis. With all their promise of flexibility and economy, these small cars should find a place in the balanced transportation systems of many communities.

WHAT'S AHEAD FOR RAILWAYS?

How old are railways? As early as the sixteenth century in England rails were laid along some cart tracks. It was found that horses could pull heavier loads if cart wheels ran smoothly along rails, avoiding ruts and potholes.

It was in 1804 that a steam-engine-powered locomotive was first tried on rails in England. That first locomotive was abandoned as too expensive, but other attempts were made. By 1825 the first daily passenger rail service in England was being offered powered by steam locomotives. The single coach, patterned after stagecoaches, carried six passengers inside and fifteen to twenty outside. It was called "The Experiment." That experiment led to rapid progress in rail travel. And for more than a hundred years it dominated the transportation field.

By the mid-1800s railway lines had been laid on every continent. Railways played an outstanding part in opening vast lands like Siberia and the western United States to settlement and development. By 1900 the United States had 260,000 miles of double steel rails. In 1950 there were almost four million miles, but by then a decline in passenger railroading had begun.

The lure of speedy air travel drew passengers away from the railways, particularly in the United States, where cross-country

Freight transport and long-distance travel were monopolized by railroads during the nineteenth century.

distances are vast—and many people are always in a hurry. For shorter trips, automobiles and buses took over.

The railways' income from passenger service dropped, but costs kept rising. Rail lines, like other public transportation systems, raised fares on the one hand and cut services and let equipment deteriorate on the other. So railway travel became less and less attractive to passengers.

Even on commuter lines serving suburbs that had grown up along the railways, the number of riders dropped. On these lines some innovations such as double-decker cars were introduced as recently as the 1950s. But more commuters drove their own cars. Fares rose and services dropped to unsatisfactory levels on these lines, too. By 1970 passenger rail service in the United States had been almost entirely abandoned as unprofitable. Many miles of the nation's vast network of tracks were being allowed to go to ruin and become overgrown by weeds.

The main lines were still busy, carrying the bulk of the heavy freight that travels overland. Freight hauling continues to be profitable, particularly for heavy goods such as coal and steel. So freight hauling methods were modernized, while passenger service was being discouraged.

Freight yards have been automatically controlled for some years. Cars have code numbers on their undersides, giving information about their ownership, load and destination. Electric "eyes" at track level pick up this information and deliver it swiftly to the control centers. Computers handle the routing and assembly of trains and record the use made of cars belonging to various companies.

Subways

Other countries, notably those of Western Europe and Japan, have modernized rail passenger service as well as freight handling. They have been far more successful in this regard than the U.S.

In many other lands underground rail lines within cities, known as subways, are as far ahead of the United States as are cross-country railways. London's Underground is efficient and comfortable. The Paris Métro is noted for its quietness as well as its scope. Mexico City has an excellent new subway in which cars travel on silent French rubber tires.

Stockholm, Berlin, and Milan have relatively new subway systems. Moscow's subway is famous for its richly decorated stations and for the depth of its tubes, reached by long, steep escalators.

Tokyo has 100 miles of subways and a short monorail line as well as some of the world's fastest intercity railway trains. The United States, because of its concentration on automobile and air travel, has fallen behind Europe and Japan in both subway construction and passenger rail service.

New Cars and Service

By the early 1970s Americans were beginning to feel an urgent need for better public transportation. Work on new subway systems was under way in several cities. And passenger service on inter-city railways began to receive thought and attention again. Europe provided some models.

One lesson that soon became clear was that government assistance or control was needed. This was true for both long-distance passenger service by rail and urban mass transit. A few key stretches of railway were chosen for a first renewal effort in the United States.

These were organized into a country-wide system called Amtrak. And the long, slow, difficult and costly rebuilding of passenger rail service began.

Equipment was in need of a great deal of modernization. New cars had to be designed that would provide more comfortable travel. These included a number of real improvements. Doorways were adapted so that handicapped people could board trains easily. New cars were designed without steep, narrow steps to climb. Wheelchairs can be rolled on and off the newest trains smoothly and can travel easily up and down the aisles. The new cars are being carpeted for comfort and quiet. Glare-free lights and window glass and air-conditioning systems provide increased comfort too.

Tracks are also being improved because most of the old roadbeds are not smooth enough to carry the new high-speed turbine-powered trains.

Some of the new trains are powered by electricity. They perform very well and are clean-running. But these cars need specially equipped track, and electrifying thousands of miles of track is an immense task.

Air-bellows springs and other rubber-bound spring systems make rides smoother and quieter. New braking systems permit travel at high speed with improved safety.

At low speeds the conventional friction brakes are more effective. But new trains are being planned to go at least 150 mph (or 250 km/h). At that speed a train needs four times as much braking power as it would need at 62.5 mph (or 100 km/h) to stop in the same distance. At high speeds the hydrokinetic brakes are invaluable.

These high-speed hydrokinetic brakes have water churning inside the brake box. When the brake is activated, energy that might have kept the train moving is turned to heating this water in the brake box. Then the hot water is transferred to the body of the car, where it cools in a radiator.

A high-speed train requires lots of extra power too. A speed of 150 mph (or 250 km/h) demands four times the power that a speed of 62.5 (or 100 km/h) requires. Speeds of 400 km/h (or 250 mph) that are already being planned for the 1990s will require 16 times the power of 160 km/h.

One way to reduce the amount of power required to move a train is to streamline it and use lightweight construction materials. Research engineers are charting moves in these directions. They know that a great deal of research and development is needed if trains and railroading are to regain the important place they once occupied in the passenger transportation field.

Hover-Trains

One plan is to equip some of the busiest passenger routes, such as Boston to New York, for hover-trains. These trains run along guide rails, but the cars are lifted above the rails on a cushion of air.

The formal name for hover-trains is Advanced Tracked Air Cushion Vehicles. The cars straddle an aluminum rail set in a concrete guideway. The guideway may be elevated above the ground level. For example, it could be raised on pylons above the route of an express highway.

It may be at ground level, perhaps following alongside a highway or railway track, for economical use of land. It may even run in a tunnel where this is necessary. Wherever the line runs, the guideways are less expensive than rails to lay. And they are much less expensive to maintain because there is no wear from friction, since no part of the car rubs against the rail in motion.

Hover-trains can attain speeds of up to 300 miles per hour, but the major obstacle to their widespread use is outdated railroad beds and tracks. (Photo courtesy of Rohr Industries)

Hover-trains have been experimentally run in Britain at 140 mph (or 225 km/h). Speeds of nearly 300 mph (or 500 km/h) are possible. But because the public seemed slow to accept the very high speeds of hover-trains, work on them was dropped in Britain in 1973.

Linear Induction Motors

Every railway needs power to run its trains. Horsepower was replaced by steam power, fueled at first by wood, then by coal and then by diesel oil. Electric power was supplied overhead to street railways and trolleys, to subways and some surface lines through a third rail. Now comes a promising new power concept, the linear induction motor.

A conventional motor, as we have seen, has a crankshaft and flywheel connected to a gear box. Their rotary motion keeps the vehicle's wheels turning. A linear induction motor, however, has no wheels or whirling parts within it. Instead, one part pushes against the other to move the train.

These motors commonly use two electromagnets. A magnet has two poles, and like poles repel each other, while unlike poles attract each other. The guide rail of the track for a linear induction system has a series of magnetized points along it. The polarization of these points is constantly changed. This means that the magnets in the base of the car are repeatedly attracted (or pulled forward) toward one magnet. Then they are repelled (or pushed away) in a forward direction. They are attracted to the next forward magnet, then repelled, and so on.

The linear induction motor provides the power for this forward motion by changing the magnetic force. At the same time, blowers in the track or in the base of the car provide an air cushion. The vehicle is suspended on this cushion just far enough above the guide rail to eliminate the rub of metal against metal that causes much of the wear and noise on conventional rail lines.

Work on these air cushions began in 1966. The idea of propelling trains by the use of magnets began to gain support in 1971. By 1973 prototype models had been built and tested. By the time you read these words, LIMs, as linear induction motors are often called, should be in operation.

A basic improvement on the noisy, heat-producing combination of steel wheels on steel rails has long been needed. Magnetic levitation, or Maglev, seems to provide an answer to that need. It promises future speeds beyond those that would be possible with steel wheels on steel rails. At 200 mph (320 km/h) steel on steel loses its gripping power. Linear induction motors with magnetic levitation have no such limitation. So they offer great promise for the future.

The Rail Pallet

Even a very swift, smooth, carefree ride on an air-cushion train will not replace for many families the convenience of using their own automobiles when they reach their destination. A new combination rail and auto service promises to provide both.

For some years a few trains have offered to carry automobiles in freight cars, while their owners rode in passenger cars. The popularity of this service, offered between New York and Florida, for example, suggested that it was worthy of some imaginative thought. The result is the rail pallet.

The rail pallet is a specially designed, electrically powered vehicle planned to run on existing tracks and on conventional wheels. The pallet cars can run individually or in trains, but they do not need locomotives. They can run forward or backward and can carry small buses, vans or automobiles.

When you are ready to travel by rail pallet, you drive onto a trackside loading platform. The car is lined up alongside the assigned pallet. The whole rounded top of the pallet will flip up, since it is hinged along the far side. And the car will be automatically moved sideways onto the pallet.

Once the vehicle is safely in place, the top of the unit will close down. You can stay in your car if you wish, working or relaxing along the way. The whole pallet will be air-conditioned, so you will be quite comfortable. And you will be freed from having to drive in traffic or bad weather. At the end of the rail trip you will have your own car ready for short trips.

This service promises to expand the use of railways so that they will once again play a major role in transporting people in the world of tomorrow.

DOWN THE RIVERS,
ACROSS THE SEAS

People have traveled by water nearly as long as they have traveled on foot. Since the first man straddled a fallen log and paddled across a stream or pond using his hands, there have been boats. Boats have been made of all sorts of materials—bundles of reeds, dugout logs, birchbark, hides, planks caulked with pitch, and more recently of iron, steel, aluminum, fiberglass and plastics.

Early boats and seagoing ships were powered by paddles, poles, oars or sails. But steam engines were put to work in boats at the same time that the engines were in land vehicles. Steam provided power

Travel on the high seas, as depicted in this illustration of 19th-century sailing vessels, still evokes a romantic, adventurous response in modern times.

that was both steadier and capable of producing more speed than the earlier devices—all of which are still in use.

The first steam-powered ship crossed the Atlantic Ocean in 1819, and regular transatlantic service was started in 1840. Smaller steamboats, often with churning paddlewheels, carried goods and people up and down great rivers even earlier. And steam-powered barges and other boats traveled the network of canals cut between rivers.

Early canal boats and river boats on their upstream journeys against the current were usually towed by teams of horses or men—and sometimes women. They were harnessed to ropes and slogged along muddy towpaths on the canal or riverbanks. Steam power freed these animals and people from that heavy drudgery.

Railways ended the great period of river and canal transport, as

Robert Fulton improved on Watt's steam engine to successfully propel river boats on the Hudson River in 1806.

planes and trucks were later to cut into the railways' place in the transportation world. In recent years bridges have largely replaced ferryboats for the crossing of rivers. Slow-moving passenger river boats have all but vanished from most waterways. And overseas airways have cut so sharply into the business of steamship lines that most passenger ships have been forced out of business.

Oceangoing ships for commercial and military uses have continued to develop, though. Turbines, which drive dynamos to power ships with electric motors, have replaced most steam engines. In the late 1950s nuclear-powered engines were installed in some large naval vessels, merchant ships and submarines.

Ships have continued to be built larger and larger. Thirty years ago ocean liners longer than a city block were considered amazing. Then battleships and aircraft carriers that were 1,000 feet long appeared. And the newest Japanese-built oil supertankers are over 1,250 feet (or about 385 meters) in length.

At the other end of the scale, small pleasure craft have been increasing steadily in numbers. New materials, such as fiberglass and plastic, have been introduced to make them lighter and more portable. There are now more than 10 million small pleasure boats in the United States. Other water-studded areas such as Scandinavia have as many as the U.S. in proportion to their population.

Perhaps because people clearly do like to be on the water some new developments in craft for public transportation by water have once again come to the fore. One of these is the hovercraft.

Over the Water

All boats and ships known to man, whatever they were made of, however they were powered, have had one thing in common. They all traveled through the water, having to push aside in waves the water they displace. That takes a great deal of energy. The hovercraft saves this energy by traveling over instead of through the water.

The hovercraft is the water-borne counterpart of the hover-train. The hover-train, described in "What's Ahead for Railways?" travels on a guide track whose walls hold in the cushion of air that supports the cars. The hovercraft replaces these guide-track walls with a "skirt" that hangs down into the water on either side of the boat. The

Commercial hydrofoils are being developed that operate smoothly even in the choppiest of waters. (Photo courtesy of Boeing Aircraft)

semi-enclosed space under the skirt contains the air cushion on which the craft rides.

Air is forced beneath the skirt by large blowers. Once the craft attains cruising speed it is pushed free of the water by this air cushion. Then it can speed along without using its power fighting the resistance of the water and making waves.

Another related above-the-water-craft, or air-cushion water vehicle, is the hydrofoil. As it pulls away from the dock, sunk low in the water of the river or bay, the hydrofoil looks rather ordinary. Passengers settle into the roomy and comfortable seats in a cabin much like that of an airliner. They arrange their hand luggage and look casually out the wide cabin windows at the slowly passing shore.

Very soon, however, the pace quickens. As the exhaust sprays foam, short metal "legs" fold out from beneath the hull and the whole craft rises from the water. Almost like a flying fish, it sails along swiftly, with only its slender foils, as the legs are called, piercing the water's surface.

The foils work much like airplane wings, lifting the hull of the craft from the water much as a plane rises from the ground when the pressure of air on the underpart of its wings exceeds that on the upper wing surfaces. The faster the craft moves, propelled by a gas-turbine engine, the less of the foils remain below the water's surface. There is very little friction between the skin of the hull and the water, so the ship does not have to use as much power as those that cut through the water instead of skimming over it. A hydrofoil can move very fast, often as much as 40 knots. (A knot is about 1.15 mph or 1.85 km/h.)

A complaint about the early hydrofoils was that they bounced a good deal when the surface was rough. Now their foils are placed at the end of long struts (pressure bars) so that the entire hull is free of the water and the foils are uniformly submerged. This permits the craft to ride smoothly even in choppy seas.

Hydrofoils have been used more in European than in North American waters. They are a common sight on the English Channel, the Danube River and the Baltic and Aegean Seas. New hydrofoils as large as big airliners are planned for other areas, though. By the time you read this book they may be in service carrying as many as 250 passengers at a time between the various islands of Hawaii, across Japan's Inland Sea, San Francisco Bay, the English Channel and along rivers and seacoasts where commuting traffic is heavy.

Sails to the Sky

However efficient the propulsion system may be, all the air-cushion ships do use irreplaceable fossil fuels, generally diesel oil. Ever since steam-powered ships took over the dominance of the seas from sailing vessels, it has been taken for granted that working ships would burn wood, coal or, in more recent decades, oil.

Steam engines and the newer turbo-electric systems have become steadily more efficient in their use of fuel. And in recent years the few nuclear-powered ships have been able to travel the seas without dipping into the dwindling stores of fossil fuels. These also save the space required for storage of bulky fuel. They avoid the necessity of stopping for refueling on a long voyage, since the uranium needed to fuel a nuclear power plant comes in very compact form. But releasing energy by splitting heavy atoms in any nuclear power plant, large or small, involves certain hazards. Rays and waste products from radioactive materials can be deadly if they should escape in case of accident. So nuclear-powered ships are unlikely to have very wide general use.

A search is still under way for alternate power sources that can be used at sea as well as on land. Solar power is getting increasing attention as a source of power on land, since the sun provides a huge amount of energy that is free and never fails.

Of course the sun shines warmly down upon the oceans of the world as well as on land. From the point of view of water transportation researchers, though, the sun's most important contribution is that it keeps the air in motion. Air in motion is wind, and the thought of wind moving over water brings us back to the idea of sailing ships.

The swift and beautiful sailing ships of old were built by men who had plenty of experience and rule-of-thumb know-how. But they had no scientific knowledge of aerodynamics, which is the interaction between the atmosphere and moving objects. Now this science has been applied to a new design in sailing ships. One experimenter has named his model the dynaship. It is still at this writing untested but is about to be put into prototype production. Other experimental work in the same direction is under way in Europe, North America and Australia.

The hull of a dynaship is quite conventional. It is planned simply to hold a large quantity of freight. But the ship's masts are quite revolutionary in design. They rise straight into the windy skies for 200 feet (more than 60 meters) without the support of the cobweb of ropes known as shrouds and stays. The horizontal yards to support the sails are of stainless steel and are curved like the ribs of airplane wings.

The sails themselves are of light, sturdy Dacron. Sailors no longer will have to scramble up into the riggings to reef or unfurl the sails.

These sails will roll out sideways from the central mast at the push of a button down on the bridge. In fact the crew of a dynaship will be very small, since the navigation and handling will be almost completely automated.

A dynaship will have four to six very tall masts, each supporting a solid bank of sails edge to edge. The masts can be pitched at different angles to the deck, and the whole mast structure can be rotated from the bridge. The broad, towering sheets of fabric mounted on these masts, which can be turned to meet each breeze, will be 60 percent more efficient than those of any previous sailing ship.

It is estimated that on the North Atlantic there are usable winds 85 percent of the time. Auxiliary engines will be needed for the rare times when the winds fail. Satellite weather reports will steer the ship's navigators around the quiet area to utilize all the available air motion.

Speed will not be the primary consideration for the dynaship. The old-fashioned, relatively slow sailing ships operated profitably on the long, slow grain routes between Australia and Great Britain until the 1920s. Some were also at work on shorter coastal runs along American shores where speed was not vital. The dynaship could be competitive in speed, though. Today's diesel-powered bulk carriers average 10 to 15 knots, and the dynaship should, according to calculations, average 12 to 16 knots.

Its most valuable advantage will be its fuel economy. There will also be a considerable saving in wages because it will use such a small crew. The fact that it offers some advantages in speed over its competitors is a welcome bonus. The dynaship will be economical, clean, quiet—and beautiful! Enthusiasts see the tall-masted, clean-rigged beauties as lively contenders for honors in transportation on tomorrow's seas.

THROUGH THE AIR

The first workable "flying machines" planned by men were paper dragons. As early as 400 B.C. the Chinese held hollow paper dragons over small fires. Hot air rises naturally, and as the hot air filled the paper shapes, they "flew" impressively high into the sky.

More than 2,000 years later, starting in 1783, this principle was applied on a larger scale. Great bags of linen and paper called *balla-oons* were filled with hot air from fires below, through openings in the bases of the balls. Some of the balloons were big enough to carry men riding in baskets slung below the inflated balls. They floated across the European countryside, sometimes with a small container of fire on board. The fire kept the air in the balloon warm, and as soon as it cooled, the craft came down.

Lighter than Air

The next step in flight was to fill balloon bags with hydrogen gas, which is lighter than air, warm or cool. This permitted the balloons to stay aloft longer.

At the end of the 1800s some balloons were enlarged, lengthened and stiffened. The baskets below them were enclosed to form comfortable cabins for crew and passengers. Gasoline engines were added to turn propellers that chewed into the air ahead, pulling ships forward. And there were rudders to steer them.

In the planning stage is a design for a 1,000-foot atomic-powered dirigible of almost unlimited range. (Photo courtesy of Goodyear)

Now the lighter-than-air craft were no longer just curiosities for sport. They were given the name of dirigibles and, since they could be driven and steered, they were put to work. They became popular in the 1920s and 1930s and even offered regularly scheduled flights across the Atlantic.

Hydrogen gas has one weakness as a fuel: It is very explosive. After several tragic dirigible explosions, the lighter-than-air ships were largely abandoned for transportation.

A few dirigibles called "blimps" continue to be used for advertising purposes, with very light and safe helium gas substituted for hydrogen as fuel. Except for the occasional advertising use and for sports such as sail-planing and hang-gliding, lighter-than-air craft seemed to have little future—until the mid-1970s.

But in the search for alternative power sources that will not devour fossil fuels and for transportation routes that will not further destroy the countryside, the helium dirigible was remembered. The dirigible may have a useful place in the field of bulky freight transport. With jet engines and sleek new aerodynamic designs, the dirigible may attain supersonic speeds.

During the decades between the 1920s and the 1970s, though, the emphasis in flight research and development concentrated on heavier-than-air craft.

Bigger, Faster, Farther

It was in 1903 that the first successful engine-powered airplane succeeded in getting off the ground and returning safely. The plane, which was made by two bicycle-builder brothers named Wright, stayed in the air for twelve seconds, traveling 100 feet (or 30 meters). This plane weighed 750 pounds (or 340 kg), including the pilot, Orville Wright. For 70 years after that first success of the Wright brothers, airplanes constantly increased in size. They also increased steadily in speed and range of flight. The length of that first flight, from take-off to landing, could be duplicated across the wings of many a present-day plane!

"Bigger, faster, higher and farther" became the watchwords of aviation. One tremendous spurt came in the 1950s, when jet planes began to appear in peacetime skies. Like so many other advances in transportation, jets had been developed for military use during World War II. They became popular for civilian use.

Earlier planes had been moved forward by propellers that bit into the air. Jets were pushed forward by the pressure of hot gases which could escape only from the rear. They provided much swifter, smoother transportation than propeller planes could achieve. Soon 500 mph (or 300 km/h) flights at altitudes above most weather disturbances were commonplace. These high altitudes provided smoother flying, but the very high speeds caused a new problem.

This problem was noise. The screaming whine of the compressor blades at the front of jet engines as the planes taxied caused many airport personnel to wear earmuffs on duty and made everyone around uncomfortable. In addition, there was the blow-torch roar from the rear of the jets on take-off, caused by the meeting of the emerging gases with the surrounding air. Homeowners for miles around the airports were in danger of acute discomfort or real damage to their hearing from the shrill intensity of the sound. Noise pollution became a new element in people's thinking about aviation.

Meanwhile, experimental planes kept pushing on toward the speed of sound. By the late 1940s the first plane had broken the sound barrier. This meant that it had traveled as fast as sound waves—750 mph (or 1200 km/h). This achievement introduced a new problem for people on the ground—the sonic boom.

Supersonic Hazards

When a plane in flight reaches the speed of sound, which is the average speed of molecules in motion, air molecules cannot get out of the way of the moving plane. They are pushed together just ahead of the nose and the leading edge of the plane's wings. A thin layer, perhaps one-tenth inch (or about 4mm) thick, of extremely dense air is formed. There is a tremendous concentration of energy in this layer, and the pressure continues to build.

As the plane pushes against this barrier of close-packed molecules, it starts a wave that resembles the V-shaped wedge that spreads out from the prow of a ship. This wave, streaming back on each side, extends out and out until it reaches the ground. There the dense band of air strikes walls and windows like a thunder clap. A good deal of damage has been reported, especially in the vicinity of military air practice ranges, caused by shock waves from planes speeding past the Mach-1 point, as the speed of sound is called.

When supersonic planes were small and relatively few, and their flights over populated areas were restricted. the damage was somewhat tolerable. Then work was begun on the construction of supersonic transport planes called SSTs, big airliners that would fly regular commercial routes. France and Britain were leaders in the field and jointly developed a model called the Concorde. The first

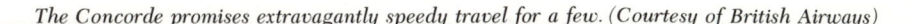

The Concorde promises extravagantly speedy travel for a few. (Courtesy of British Airways)

Concordes flew in 1969. They did not prove to be economically practical since they could carry relatively small passenger loads.

The United States government also supported the development of an SST in the 1960s. But so many objections were raised by people concerned about possible environmental damage that in 1971 money to support this project was cut off by the Congress.

Increased noise pollution, particularly near airports, was one threat of the SSTs. Sonic booms were another. Possible effects of the jet emissions on the composition of the stratosphere were a third major concern. Some scientists claimed that the emission of gases into the thin stratosphere might change the patterns of travel of solar energy to earth. These changes might lead to harm to both plant and animal life.

For example, jet emissions appear to cut down the amount of ozone (O_3) in the stratosphere. Ozone molecules absorb many ultraviolet rays of sunlight on their way to earth. If they came through in too great numbers, serious problems such as an increase in skin cancer from sunburning might result.

Some recent studies indicate that this fear was based largely on faulty calculations. So the advocates of the SST hope that when tests and checks have been completed opposition to the speedy planes may lessen.

SSTs are admittedly not efficient users of fuel, but the principal remaining objections are to sonic booms and excessive noise. As to sonic booms, supporters of the supersonic transports promise that the planes would fly mainly over oceans and would not reach supersonic speeds over inhabited land areas. Forecasters promise rockets that will hurl silent unpowered planes into the stratosphere, where they will glide for great distances. To deal with the excessive noise of today and tomorrow, experiments in the field of airplane design are under way. Let us see what they promise.

Pivoting Wings

The small plane seems to stagger under the buffeting of an unearthly wind. Its wings have been swept around at a strange angle to the fuselage, forward on one side, back on the other.

Actually the plane is a model being tested in a supersonic wind tunnel. In the tunnel the airplane model, with force-measuring

Two overlapping models developed by NASA's Advanced Transport Technology program display the difference in wing sweep between a Mach 0.98 aircraft on top of a Mach 0.90 plane beneath. (Photo courtesy of Bruce Frisch)

devices inside it, remains stationary on its supporting bar. The air rushes by it at the speed at which a real airplane might rush through the air. And the effect on the model plane is the same as if it were flying at high speed.

The plane being tested is one proposed to diminish the noise and improve the economy of supersonic flight. A cruising speed of Mach 1.4 seems the maximum that will permit the use of a relatively quiet fan jet engine. This engine cuts noise by changing the "mix" as the jet emissions meet the surrounding air. What is being tested here is the turnable wing.

Delta wings, swept back from the straight horizontal to a triangular shape, have been used before on high-speed planes. Some designers feel that the most effective wing form for supersonic transports will be in the traditional elliptical shape. But it will be designed to turn in flight as a unit to angles of 45 to 60 degrees to the fuselage instead of remaining at the conventional 90 degrees.

The elliptical shape cuts wave drag. Wave drag is a mass of waves (energy) going away from the plane. These waves appear as soon as the plane has passed the speed of sound. Wave drag can start on certain points like the fuselage or the leading edge of the wing. It generally increases with speed, though not always regularly. Rotating the wing cuts the drag and therefore increases the efficiency of the plane.

Landings and take-offs would be made at relatively low speeds. For these the wing would remain in the traditional 90-degree position. For flights over land, where speed must be kept low enough to avoid sonic booms, the wing would be turned, while in the air, to about a 45-degree angle. For overwater flights at speeds of Mach 1.4 or more, the angle would be about 60 degrees.

Before this one-piece wing was thought of, "swing wings" were considered. They pivoted back from the fuselage on either side. This placed a great strain on the pivots. In addition, when the wings were swept back the center of lift was displaced toward the rear of the plane, throwing it badly off balance.

The new model seems to overcome these weaknesses. Its single wing is much stronger than a pair of wings attached by pivots to the fuselage. The fuselage itself can be kept at its most streamlined, cylindrical shape. With one side of the wing turning forward while the other side swings back, the balance of the plane is not disturbed.

To the Airport by Air

As the flying time between large cities is shortened, it seems to take longer and longer to get to and from the airports. On many flights passengers spend as much time traveling to and from the airports as they do in the air.

As with most major problems, this one has more than one factor contributing to it. One is the congestion of traffic in most cities. The automobile and bus are still the most frequently used vehicles between town and airport in the mid-1970s. Both operate on crowded highways and streets where delays are common.

Another contributor to delays is the distance from the central city at which most modern airports have to be located. Larger, faster planes need longer runways for landings and take-offs. Increasing numbers of flights demand more space for runways, plane parking, gates and other terminal facilities, as well as automobile parking. The amount of land needed for a major new airport simply cannot be found close to a large city. Objections to the noise of planes coming and going at a big airport provide another reason for locating them farther from the city, not to mention avoiding the risk of possible crashes in heavily populated sections.

Many people want service by air from downtown locations to major airports. They are tired of the slowness of bus and car service. And they do not see the high-speed commuter trains, the "people movers" and monorails that a few cities have tried as the solution for them. So a good deal of research is under way to find a plane that can serve effectively for these short but important stages of longer air journeys.

The most promising planes for this use are short-take-off-and-landing aircraft known as STOLs. They are still at this writing in the experimental stage. As their name suggests, STOLs will need only short runways for take-offs and landings. So they could come and go from small airports that might be located in the central city. They could operate in the 50- to 500-mile range. Most of their service would be flying passengers to large regional airports.

A STOLport was planned a few years ago to float on the East River beside Manhattan. But residents in the nearby neighborhood protested against the noise they feared it would cause. Tests were made that showed that the quietest streets of the area were already noiser than the level of sound that would reach them from the STOLport. The noisiest streets of the neighborhood were already noisier than the edge of the airport itself would be. So the addition of the airport would make practically no difference in the noise level. This gloomy news did not reconcile the neighbors, though. The plan had to be abandoned.

Research aeronautical engineers realize that a plane that can land on and take off from short runways solves only part of their problem. They must also provide a really quiet plane, since its job will be to land near centers of population. And they must provide a pleasantly smooth ride for passengers although these short-run planes must fly at low altitudes where the air is often turbulent. Quiet and stability are the aims of a great deal of present-day research.

A dynamically scaled model of the short-take-off-and-landing concept has been prepared for free-flight investigations of the stability and control characteristcs of the aircraft. (Photo by NASA staff photographer Robert E. Nye)

Wind-tunnel tests of experimental models suggest that progress is being made. One model featuring the augmentor wing will help cut noise by placing a shield to break the path of sound waves toward the ground. This model will also mix the jet flow with air before it is emitted from the plane. The process lowers the velocity of the gas as it strikes the air. This is important because the meeting of gas and air is what causes the jet screech.

Another promising model is planned to avoid both noise and stability problems. It has swept-back wings with double- or triple-slotted flaps. These flaps will "blow out" behind the wings to increase the plane's lift. The engines are placed close to the fuselage under the wings, so the exhaust gases are caught by the flaps, which lessens the noise. The tail is unusually large and high-mounted to provide improved stability and control. This lessens the chance of uncomfortable rolling in rough air.

The STOL models show promise. But some experts point out that there is already in service an aircraft that offers speed, reliability, flexibility in size and all-weather capability. It requires only 5 percent as much landing space as the STOL! This aircraft is the helicopter, which can take off and land straight up and down.

Helicopter service is available from New York area airports directly to the roofs of some business buildings in Manhattan. Service is also available between the several New York area airports and between other major airports such as Los Angeles and San Francisco and their nearby communities. Though the "choppers," which like most aircraft were developed primarily for military purposes, are noisier and use more fuel than is desirable, it seems likely that they will be more widely used in the near future. Research efforts will almost certainly bring improvements in their performance.

Tomorrow and Tomorrow

Space travel has not been mentioned, because the day when it will be available to the general public is farther off than the "tomorrow" of which we have been speaking. But it is probable that lessons learned from space flights will be applied to air travel within the atmosphere in ways that are not yet clear.

During the decades just past the main thrusts in air travel have been toward higher, faster and longer flights. Now that people are giving more thought to the values of quiet, tranquility and pure air, and now that we realize that our bodily mechanisms simply do not operate well if we rush through too many time zones rapidly, our aims are shifting. Size and speed no longer seem such great goals. It may be that tomorrow's surprise breakthrough in air travel may not be a bigger, faster passenger plane to hurtle hundreds of people through the air at more than the speed of sound. It may instead be something as small as one- or two-passenger flying platforms to free pedestrian travelers from the crowding of city streets.

Only one thing in the future is definite: there will be major changes in transportation on land, water and in the air. For the human race is a restless, inquisitive, puzzle-solving lot, and research and experimentation are on the move on countless fronts.

3 COMMUNICATION:

To Keep in Touch

A hundred years or so ago, if you wanted to talk with someone you walked or rode (usually on horseback or in a horse-drawn carriage) to see that person. And you talked face to face. If you could not travel, you took pen in hand—possibly a pen fashioned from a sharpened goose quill—dipped it in ink colored with lampblack and wrote out the message. Records in offices were kept the same way, written out slowly by longhand.

A letter traveled by railway a century ago. But not long before that letters and newspapers were carried in saddlebags on horseback or by horse-drawn mail coach.

Some faster ways of sending brief messages had been in use for hundreds, even thousands of years. Usually these techniques were used only for official messages, simplified to a code. Code signals were sent by means of beaten drums, waved flags or shifted semaphore arms. Signal fires conveyed messages at night or on a clear day. But personal communication at a distance was extremely slow and scant.

The Telegraph and Telephone

It was in the first half of the nineteenth century that the modern age of communication began. By then electricity had come into limited use. It was known that electric current flowed through wires when a circuit was closed or completed. When the circuit was broken, the current stopped flowing. In 1832 Samuel F. B. Morse used the rapid breaking of a circuit with a small switch called a key to send messages as far as wires could be stretched. And he developed a code alphabet for the purpose. The first long-distance message was dispatched by this method in 1844.

Before many years had passed, the Morse code was standard for sending messages by wire. Dots (brief spurts of current) and dashes (longer) in various combinations stand for all the letters of the alphabet and the basic numbers. Both the Morse code and the telegraph are still in use. But a telegram delivered from the telegraph office to a home is, although faster than a letter, still expensive and slow. It is usually reserved for urgent messages, often bad news.

In 1876 Alexander Graham Bell demonstrated that the human voice could be carried over wires. In addition to being valuable in business, the Bell telephone brought a whole new form of social life into countless homes where women, the elderly or shut-ins had spent many lonely days. Now at the turn of a crank and the lifting of a receiver, they could speak to the local operator and then to a friend.

Today telephone calls are used to discuss business deals, homework assignments, parties, sports and innumerable other topics on a person-to-person basis. Telephone communication has made it easier for us to be in touch with people of similar interests.

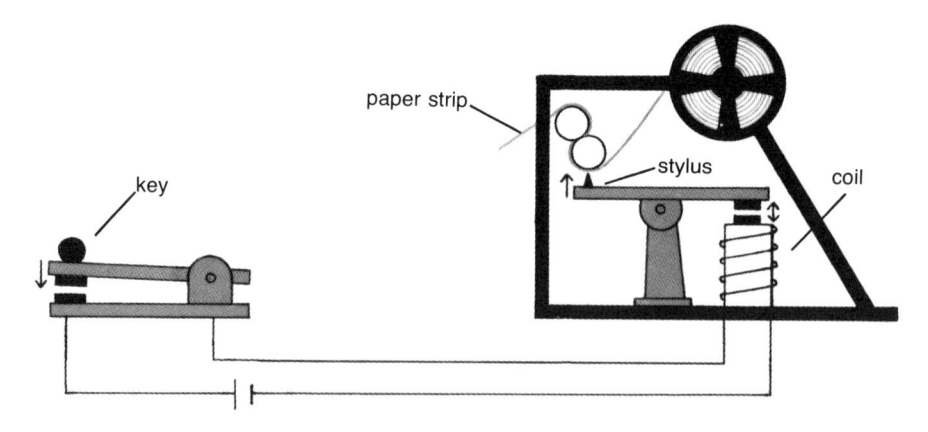

Pressure on the key of this early telegraph set closed the electric circuit so the magnetized coil attracted the lever at left, sending the stylus point up to mark a code of dots and dashes developed by Morse onto the paper strip.

Public Communication

Until the beginning of the twentieth century, anyone who wanted to communicate ideas, spread information or stimulate, entertain or amuse people had to write a newspaper article, book or pamphlet, go on a lecture tour or on the stage or perform in a friend's parlor.

By 1900 new possibilities were emerging. The phonograph had been invented by Thomas Edison, and it was becoming popular in the home-entertainment field. Musical groups and comedians were making recordings, and playing of these recordings enlivened many quiet evenings at home. One had only to crank up a turntable, place a grooved record on it and lower an arm so that the metal or sharpened wooden needle attached to the arm lightly touched the turning record. As the record turned one could hear opera singers, symphony orchestras or comedians, all without leaving home. In turn, artists and entertainers had a new outlet for communicating with a greatly expanded public.

Next came the radio. It started in 1901 as an extension of the telegraph. Then Guglielmo Marconi demonstrated transatlantic wireless telegraphy, using electromagnetic waves.

At first the wireless could carry only dot-dash or "on-off" messages. But by the early 1920s broadcasting of voices and music had been developed, and home receivers for these wave messages were available. Broadcasting meant turning sound waves into electrical patterns and imposing those patterns on electromagnetic waves in a radio transmitter. The transmitter then sent these waves out for anyone to receive. To receive the waves there must be a receiving set that is tuned to the proper frequency within the range of the transmitter. The sound-wave pattern carried by the radio waves is turned back into sound waves in the receiver, and the words and music can then be heard.

By the early 1920s many homes had small crystal-set radios with earphones attached. One person at a time could listen to music or voices being broadcast miles away. Then sets with loudspeakers made it possible for several people to listen together without the cumbersome earphones.

As radios broadcasting and receiving equipment developed in clarity and power, it brought into countless homes a great store of information and entertainment. News was broadcast as it was happening. Entertainment ranged from comedy to opera and classical music. But to see entertainment as well as hear it, one still had to go to a theater or concert hall.

Television was invented in the 1940s, adding a picture to the sound. In the past 30 years television has revolutionized the entertainment industry as well as the world of news-gathering and distribution. It is also changing education.

Radio is still widely used for person-to-person communication on the "ham-radio" frequencies as well as for public broadcasting. Television, however, has been almost entirely a medium for mass communication. Closed-circuit television is now being developed to reach special audiences but person-to-person television has not yet become commonplace.

Communications, both private and public, are expanding and changing rapidly. It is worthwhile to look at some of the areas in which these developments are taking place, for they will have a vast influence on ways of living in the years to come.

CHANNELS OF COMMUNICATION

Most of our communication channels depend on the motion of unseen waves. When we speak to one another we communicate through sound waves that travel through the air from us to cause the hearer's eardrums to vibrate. When we talk to others by telephone or radio, electrical or electromagnetic waves carry our messages.

Sound waves do not travel very far. Even the loudest thunder claps cannot be heard more than a few miles away. Telegraph and telephone messages can be carried to great distances, but as electrical currents flowing through wires or as electromagnetic waves traveling through space rather than as sound waves. Sometimes these waves move through special cables or wave guides.

To understand how these various methods function, it will be necessary to review some basic principles.

Telephone

When you speak into a telephone, the sound waves emitted by your voice press against a thin metal diaphragm inside the transmitter. The air pressure changes with each rise and fall of your voice, and the diaphragm vibrates to each change. The vibration, in turn, changes the pressure on a cluster of carbon granules behind the diaphragm. And the shifting of the carbon changes the electrical resistance between the two terminals.

1877   *1907*   *1919*

Three stages in the development of the telephone: The first commercial telephone (left) had a cameralike opening that served as both transmitter and receiver; the magneto wall set (center) had a built-in generator for signaling the operator; and the dial telephone (right), which was invented in 1892 but was not widely used until its complex equipment was better developed in the early 20th century. (Photos courtesy of Bell Laboratories)

A steady electrical voltage is applied to these terminals. The rising and falling tones of your voice produce a matching fluctuation in the electrical current. This current, with all its fluctuations, travels along wires until it reaches a telephone receiver. There it causes an electromagnet to attract another thin diaphragm with the same fluctuating force. This causes the diaphragm in the receiver to set up a pattern of sound waves similar to those you sent into the transmitter. And your friend hears "the sound of your voice."

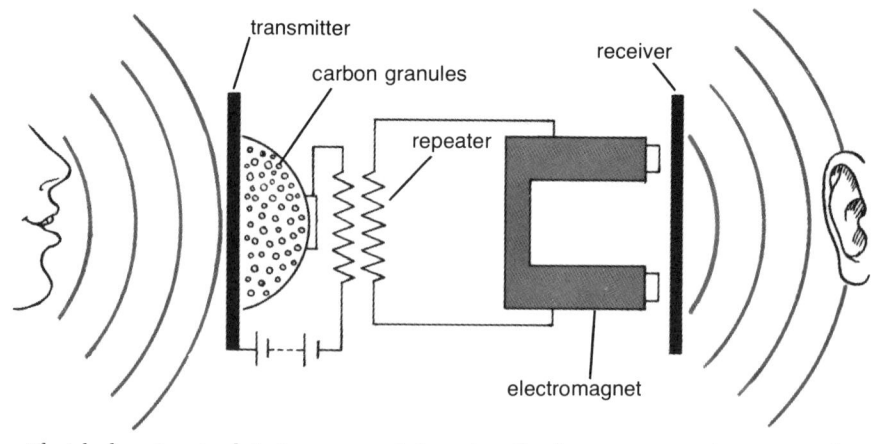

The telephone is a simple instrument consisting primarily of a transmitter and a receiver. The sound waves are received in the transmitter and converted to electrical impulses, which are changed back into sound waves in the receiver.

Telephones have provided a means of sending voice messages across distances for a hundred years. Advances in telecommunication have been almost continuous. Messages are now carried by radio waves or via cables laid on ocean floors or reflected from satellites. The principle of the telephone, however, remains much as it was a century ago.

The earliest telephone instruments each used a pair of wires. As the use of telephones expanded, separate pairs of wires for each call became impractical. The skeins of individual wires dangling above city streets were unsightly and unsafe. Cables containing many pairs of twisted wires tightly packed together have now come into use. In mid-city areas they are almost always buried underground. In the suburbs and countryside, they often are carried overhead on poles.

Make It Louder

The earliest telephone calls could travel only about twenty miles before loss of volume made them inaudible. It was the electron or vacuum tube that first amplified the very faint current set up by a human voice so that it could travel across long distances.

Today the transistor has largely replaced the vacuum tube as an amplifier. In vacuum tubes electrons travel through space. Transistors use special solid materials instead of space. These materials, called semiconductors, are in the form of crystals. Electrons travel through infinitesimal holes in the crystals. As in vacuum tubes, the flow of large currents through these crystals is controlled by smaller currents. So the signals carried by the small currents are amplified.

These tiny transistors have special value because they are small, light and use very little power. A transistor can be operated on the power of a tiny battery—as little as 1/100,000 of a watt. They can even be fitted into small hearing aids to amplify sound signals there.

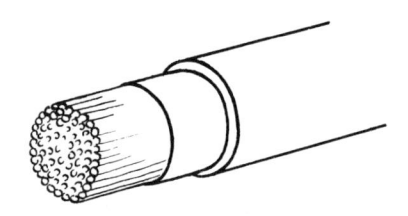

Cables containing many pairs of twisted wires tightly packed together are now in common use.

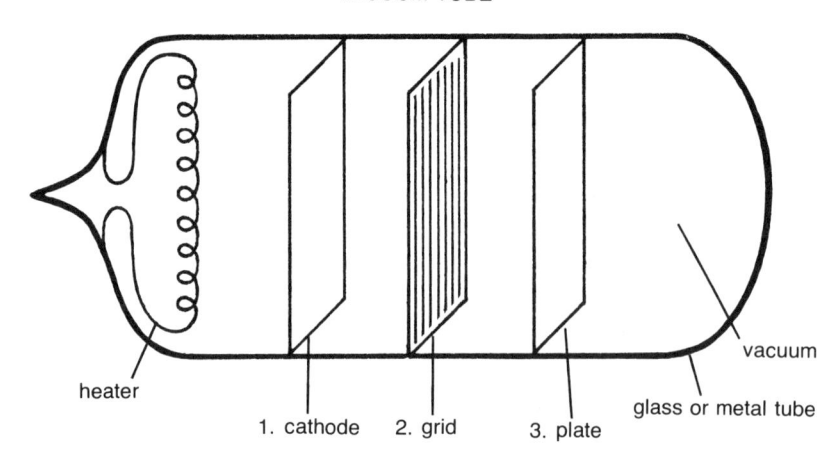

VACUUM TUBE

heater
1. cathode   2. grid   3. plate   vacuum   glass or metal tube

The vacuum tube is like a valve, operated by a very small electrical current, which controls the passage of a larger current. The principal elements of a single vacuum tube are: 1) a hot filament (or cathode) from which electrons are boiled off; 2) a wire grid that receives the tiny electric voltage variations carrying voice or music signals; 3) a plate to which the boiled-off electrons are attracted. The number of electrons (−) that are attracted to the plate (+) and go on to be converted back into sound depends on the grid voltage. The voltage on the grid varies with the sound signal it carries. So the grid passes on all its variations to the plate in the form of electrons—in other words, the voice pattern. The current reaching the plate is much stronger than the original voice current. So the voice pattern is sent along its way in a much strengthened or amplified form.

In the transmission of most long-distance calls across land, transistors are invaluable for building up signals. The messages that travel by wire must go through repeater stations. These are built in at regular intervals. When vacuum tubes were used, the cable fitted with tubes bulged every few miles. Each bulge marked another repeater station to step up the power of the voice signal. In the newest cables, small transistors serve the same purpose with very little bulging. Thanks to these repeater stations with tubes or transistors, signals can travel thousands of miles in an instant, to emerge in the pattern of familiar voices.

Most transcontinental telephone service is still by wire and cable. But today's long-distance systems are making increasing use of radio lanes. Use of these invisible electromagnetic waves for sending messages is the key to the story of tomorrow's communication systems, to be discussed in the following pages.

Wireless Telephony

Overseas telephone service by radio was tried as early as 1923. Radiophone was the earliest kind of overseas telephone service. It was not very satisfactory because it was expensive and the resulting connection was often noisy and weak. Today communication satellites circle the earth. The satellites receive signals beamed from the ground, amplify them and send the signals along to their destination. There the signal arrives clear and recognizable.

Over land, systems of microwave repeater stations are used to "hop" radio signals from one station to the next. An antenna at the dispatch end shoots out its signals—not broadcast, as with ordinary radio, but carefully narrowed into a directional beam. About thirty miles away or as far as possible without being hidden below the curve of the horizon, the antenna of a repeater station picks up the beam. The signal is amplified by transistors or vacuum tubes and sent on its way.

These radio lanes save the expense of installing and maintaining elaborate systems of wires. But they do require stations located on high buildings, mountains or tall towers to keep the number of relays as low as possible.

Coaxial cables are also used to carry telephone—and television—signals. Electromagnetic waves are carried inside copper tubes, actually in the space between the tube and a wire running down its center. Often wire and coaxial cable circuits are combined by placing a number of pairs of wires in the same bundle with as many as twenty coaxial cables. As many as 2,700 two-way telephone conversations can be carried in one of these cables.

Hollow wave guides, which are rather like coaxial cables without the central wire, can also carry radio waves. One guide can accommodate as many as 250,000 two-way telephone conversations!

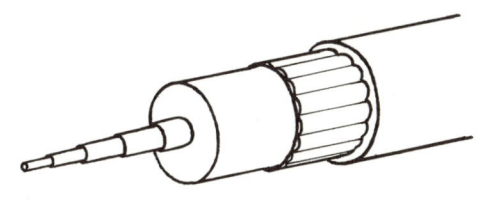

Coaxial cable for use under the ocean has a copper cylinder containing copper conductors with polyethylene insulation.

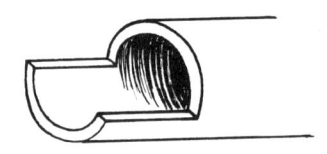

This wave guide is a tube about 7.5 cm in diameter that can carry 250,000 two-way voice channels.

These varied services combine to make it possible for any of the world's more than 250 million telephones to be connected with any other—though for many of the callers to understand one another's languages presents quite another problem!

Radio Amateurs

Using a telephone system to send a message does not satisfy some people. They want a more individual kind of service, under their own control. Since the early days of radio some of these people have enjoyed building and operating radio transmitters and receivers as a hobby. These radio amateurs, known as "hams," visit with one another, discuss their radio equipment and often handle messages to all parts of the world as a service to the public. They are not allowed to charge for handling these messages. But often when storms or earthquakes have disabled telephone lines, ham stations have provided the only contact with the outside world for isolated communities.

Ham operators must pass examinations to prove that they understand radio technology and law before they are granted licenses to operate their radio transmitters. Many important new ideas about radio communication have been developed by these amateurs. In their effort to send and receive messages across the longest possible distances as clearly and economically as possible, hams have built new kinds of antennas, receivers and transmitters. They are always willing to try something new, even if it theoretically won't work. Sometimes the theory has been proven wrong. Then the scientists have to revise the theories to account for the new facts the hams have discovered.

Many electronics engineers of today started as ham radio

operators. Their interest has been instrumental in the development of equipment such as mobile telephones.

Mobile Telephones

Many of our important community services now depend on the mobile radio-telephone sets carried in automobiles or trucks. These have made police cars, fire trucks, ambulances, taxicabs and service trucks more useful and efficient. Their crews can remain in touch with central stations even when they cannot be reached by land-line telephone service.

Since the transistor became available, radio receivers and two-way radio sets have been built to be carried easily in a pocket or worn on a belt. You step into a taxi and give the driver the address to which you want to go. He will pick up a small microphone, give his name and tell his office where he is and where he is going. Call for a tow truck and the nearest one will be contacted by mobile telephone. Report a situation that calls for police intervention. Officers cruising nearby in a squad car will hear their call numbers and a message saying something like "A 211 at 116 Elm Street."

Thousands of individuals have radio telephones in their private automobiles hooked into the public telephone network via radio.

The main problem is that many subscribers must share the few radio channels that are available for this service. All too often someone on the channel insists on talking for a long time. This distresses someone else who is waiting to make—or to receive—an important call.

A new portable telephone comes in a neat 28-ounce package. This unit includes mouthpiece, transmitter, earphone, bell and push-button keyboard for calling in the number. The number signal is transmitted over FM radio frequencies to the nearest of a chain of transmitter-receivers. From there it goes into the telephone network. Calls can be received on this portable telephone by the same steps in reverse.

Citizens' Band Radio

Within the past two decades some radio channels have been set aside for the use of the general public. This "citizens' band" equipment is used to control model airplanes and boats, to open garage doors, for conversations between people in automobiles and their homes or offices, between people in two moving automobiles or trucks and between hand-held "walkie-talkies."

These gadgets have become very popular. Anyone who has listened to a citizens' band receiver will agree that these channels are greatly overloaded, with too many people often trying to talk at once on the same frequency.

One expert forecasts that the next revolution in communication, will be in the field of sending of person-to-person messages. To understand what some of these advances may be, it will be well to take a closer look at the range of waves in the electromagnetic spectrum.

Some experts predict that the next revolutionary advance in communications will be in sending of person-to-person messages by means such as this mobile telephone.

THE LONG AND SHORT OF WAVES

The wide range of electromagnetic waves that travel through space includes radio waves, heat, light and X rays. A rainbow is a vivid display of one small part of this wide spectrum—the part that is visible to us as light. At one edge of the rainbow we see red light. These waves have the lowest frequency and longest wavelength our eyes can see. At the other edge of the rainbow are the indigo and violet colors—the highest frequency and shortest waves we can see.

The frequency of a wave is simply the number of complete waves or cycles that pass a given point in one second. Frequency is often expressed as cycles per second (cps); however, the scientific term for one cycle per second is one hertz (hz). Radio waves are often called hertzian waves, in honor of Heinrich Hertz, who was responsible for much of the understanding of them.

The number of waves to pass a given point in one second depends both on the length of each wave and on the speed at which it travels. One equation is used for all electromagnetic waves: Velocity equals frequency times wavelength, or $v = fw$. The velocity of all electromagnetic waves is the same. It is the speed of light, 300,000 km/sec. Thus a radio wave whose frequency is 3,000,000 hz (or 3 megahertz) has a wavelength of 0.1 km (1,000 meters), since, to turn

the equation around, $w = v/f$ or $\dfrac{300,000 \text{ km/sec.}}{3,000,000 \text{ hz.}}$

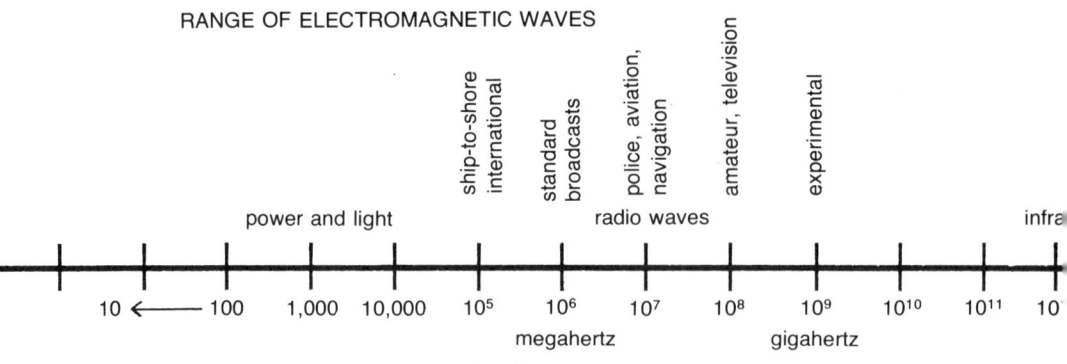

RANGE OF ELECTROMAGNETIC WAVES

Numbers = frequency cycles per sound, or Hertz

Electromagnetic waves are produced in many different ways. Radio and television stations, for example, have large transmitters. These generate radio and TV signals that are sent into space through antennas. These signals are then picked up by our radio and TV antennas and turned back into music or pictures by our receiving sets.

These stations operate on channels that are assigned to them by national government agencies. Since electromagnetic waves travel long distances and do not recognize political boundaries, there are also international treaties governing some of these channel assignments. These treaties represent one of the best examples of how nations can work together over the years and agree on the use of a valuable natural resource—in this instance, the electromagnetic spectrum. It is worthwhile considering the nature and value of this resource, because its wise use is a challenge to the lawmakers and administrators of nations today and in our world tomorrow.

The Range of Waves

All electromagnetic waves travel through space at the same velocity, but waves of different frequencies behave quite differently when they encounter air, water or a solid material.

We all know that X rays, with the highest frequency and shortest wavelength of all electromagnetic waves, can travel through our bodies. The shadows on an X ray picture show that X rays pass through bones less readily than through skin or muscular tissue.

Following X rays on the electromagnetic spectrum of frequencies are light waves. Our eyes cannot see all light waves. The sun emits

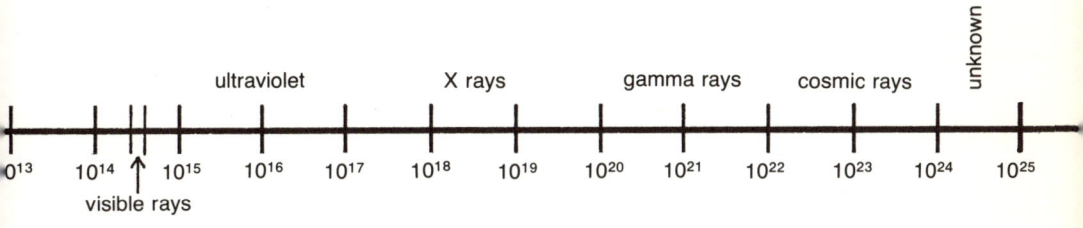

about 10 billion trillion kilowatts of power. The earth receives continuously almost 20 trillion kilowatts of this power from the sun. But much of this enormous power is in the ultraviolet end of the spectrum that we cannot see. We can feel it, for our skins sunburn or become tanned from the small fraction of ultraviolet waves that manage to pass through all the earth's atmosphere and reach us. Similarly, air, water and soil are warmed by the infrared rays from the sun, which are at the other end of the light spectrum and are too low in frequency for us to see.

The radio-frequency portion of the electromagnetic spectrum begins at the lower (red) end of the light waves, at about 300 billion hertz (300 gigahertz), and extends all the way down to 30 hertz. Thus the highest radio frequency is 10 billion times the lowest, and the ratio of the longest to the shortest radio wavelength is also 10 billion to one. Over this vast range radio waves differ widely in the way they travel. And quite different kinds of equipment are required to make them all usable.

Present-day research is centered mainly on frequencies at the top of the radio-frequency spectrum, though some attention is also being focused on those at the low end. The medium frequency (MF) band, from 30,000 to 3,000,000 hertz (30 to 3,000 kilohertz), is already being very intensively used.

The broadcast stations you can receive on your portable transistor radio are found in the MF band, which tunes from 550 to 1,600 khz.

Frequencies and transmitter power output in the MF band are regulated through international treaties because MF waves bend around the surface of the earth in the daytime and are reflected from the earth's ionosphere at night. This means that the signals travel across very long distances, particularly at night. So stations hundreds of miles away could interfere with the reception of nearby broadcasts if "clear channels" were not assigned through international agreements.

Another familiar use of the radio spectrum is found in the very high frequency (VHF) band, from 30 to 300 million hertz (30 to 300 megahertz). Here are found twelve television channels (those numbered from 2 to 13), all of the FM broadcast stations and many of the police, fire, taxicab and aircraft channels. VHF waves are bent only a little by the earth and its atmosphere, so this band is used for line-of-sight signals. Central VHF antennas are usually located on mountaintops, tall buildings or towers, so that the line of sight extends as far as possible.

Frequencies at the low end of the radio spectrum are used for long-distance communications, because they are bent by the earth's ionosphere and can travel very far beyond the horizon. Ships, submarines and aircraft use the low frequency (LF) band, 30 to 300 khz, and very low frequency (VLF) band, 3 to 30 khz, to keep in touch with land stations and to operate radio-navigation systems. These frequencies are subject to interference from lightning storms and from sunspot activity—which reaches a peak every eleven years—so they are not always usable.

The VHF band came into use for TV channels, FM broadcast stations, police cars, fire trucks, military services and taxicabs just after World War II. The demand for channels soon caused many problems for the governmental regulatory agencies because there were not enough channels for everyone who wanted them. Now engineers have designed equipment capable of operating at still higher frequencies, which has made many more channels available.

The band above the VHF range is ultra-high frequency (UHF), from 300 to 3,000 megahertz (300 mhz to 3 gigahertz). Most of the technology for using the UHF band came from wartime development of radar. In this UHF band authorities have been able to assign another 70 TV channels and many additional channels for police, fire, aircraft, citizens' band and taxicab use.

Many of our satellites use this band, as does some of the radar equipment that guides aircraft and ships. With all these uses, even the UHF band is overcrowded.

Above 3 gigahertz lies the superhigh frequency (SHF) or microwave region. Because microwaves have such short wavelengths, they can be focused, like a searchlight, by using large reflectors as part of the antennas. Microwave beams are used for line-of-sight transmission of signals carrying telephone messages, television and computer data. One beam can, for example, reach from an antenna on top of a truck parked outside a football stadium to another antenna atop a tall building or mountain to carry the TV picture and sound to the station that broadcasts it. The same picture and sound can be relayed to other high mountains or towers for the repeated "hops" that enable people across the country to enjoy the football game. Between New York and Los Angeles, for example, 107 relay stations are used.

Since 1964 satellites have vastly extended the line-of-sight distance for microwave transmission. From a height of 22,000 miles a satellite can receive a signal originating on earth and relay it back to a point almost halfway around the globe. Satellites can now bring newsworthy events in distant lands to our home TV sets as they are actually happening.

The demand for additional channels still continues to grow. The next step will be the use of light waves for carrying messages. We shall see in the next chapter how light waves can carry enormous numbers of messages and why they are destined to play a very important part in the life of tomorrow's communities.

After several unsuccessful tries, COMSAT Intelsat IV communications satellite was placed in orbit over the Atlantic in 1970. It handles 9,000 telephone circuits simultaneously. (Photo courtesy of American Telephone and Telegraph)

SENDING WORDS AND PICTURES

Different kinds of messages require electromagnetic highways of different widths on which to travel. Sending a telegram by spelling out the message letter by letter with a hand-operated telegraph key requires only a narrow electromagnetic pathway or, in engineering terms, a narrow bandwidth. A skillful operator can open and close the key ten times a second, sending ten bits of information per second. In general, each bit per second requires one hertz (or cycle per second) of bandwidth. Transmitting a telegram by radio channel thus requires a band 10 hertz wide.

When we speak into a telephone our voices cause the diaphragm to vibrate at frequencies from 300 hz to about 4,000 hz. The bandwidth needed for transmitting voice messages is thus about 3,700 hz. Often, to save bandwidth in our increasingly crowded channels, telephone circuits are only about 3,000 hz wide. This makes voices often sound somewhat unnatural, but they are still quite understandable and usually recognizable.

Musical instruments generate frequencies from 15 or 20 hz up to 15,000 hz or more, and a healthy human ear can hear frequencies up to 15,000 or even 20,000 hz. High-fidelity music channels therefore require bandwidths of at least 15,000 hz.

Television pictures and computer data require the broadest electromagnetic highways. A TV channel may be as much as 6

This is a scene at a TV operating center in New York City that transmits network radio and television programs throughout the world. (Photo courtesy of Bell Telephone)

megahertz wide. (A megahertz is a million cycles per second.) A high-speed computer requires a "superhighway" to send data bits to another high-speed computer.

Television Transmission

In a television camera, light from the scene being photographed passes through the lens and knocks electrons off a sensitive screen. These electrons travel to a plate where they form again to make an invisible electron image of the scene. The picture is broken up into tiny dots in lines across the screen. There are 324 dots per horizontal line and 525 lines on the grid of the screen. The whole image is scanned to form waves of electrical current. The waves vary with the

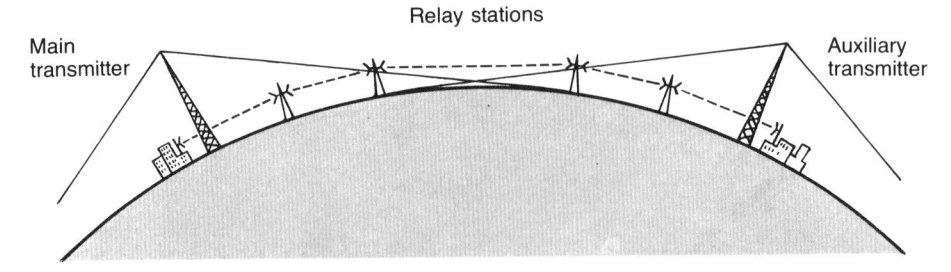

Television is transmitted via microwaves that do not bend, so it must follow line-of-sight paths.

amount of light in each of the tens of thousands of dots. This current is amplified and sent to the transmitter.

A fine electron beam traces this whole pattern thirty times a second, so rapidly that the human eye sees the picture as a continuous whole when it is reproduced in the receiving set. The rays enter an electron gun at the back of the picture tube. A stream of electrons from this gun strikes the chemical coating inside the front of the picture tube. There it recreates the pattern of light and dark—or color—that entered the lens of the camera back in the TV studio. Only rarely, when something goes wrong, does a shifting pattern of meaningless dots—called "snow"—appear on the receiving screen.

A television broadcast needs a band nearly six million hertz wide compared to 3,700 for a telephone conversation. The actual channel bandwidth usually provided is a little less than the high-fidelity bandwidth. About 4.5 mhz provides a picture we find acceptable for good viewing. For a very small picture, a bandwidth as narrow as 2.5 mhz is satisfactory.

Actually only a small part of most pictures changes each one-thirtieth of a second. If only the changes are transmitted, a much narrower bandwidth can be used. But the equipment to do this is so complex and expensive that it is as yet seldom used.

Computer data links often reduce the bandwidth needed by sending information so slowly that ordinary telephone circuits can transmit the message. Where high-speed data transmission is really needed, it must have costly extra bandwidth.

Telephone companies have equipment to make the most efficient possible use of channel bands. One kind of special equipment monitors for unused channel time and slips other messages into the gaps, since we are actually speaking only a fraction of the time we use a long-distance telephone circuit. Occasionally we hear a bit of these overlapping messages in the background of our conversation.

Techniques for reducing the needed bandwidth have helped reduce the cost of sending messages or information, because narrow channels are cheaper than broad ones, just as a narrow road is less expensive to build and maintain than a wide highway.

More Channels

There is a growing demand for more channels, particularly in the television range. Actually 82 channels have been assigned to television broadcasts in the United States. But 70 of these are in the ultra-high frequency range, where the reception distance is shorter than for the 12 channels in the very-high-frequency range.

Utilizing many more of the available broadcast channels would increase the variety of programs that could be offered on television. With only a few commercial channels, each one must attract a huge audience to justify very high charges for advertising time. Costs for producing programs, as well as for transmission, are very large. The major networks feel that they must try to keep the appeal of their programs at a middle range to try to meet the median of viewers' tastes. The result is programs that generally do not rival in quality the best of books, theater, art or music.

With more channels utilized, however, programs could be directed to small special-interest audiences. This would be desirable, but it is not simple. The problem is that the costs of production and transmission must still be covered.

These extremely high costs do not apply to the use of closed-circuit television for broadcasting lectures or experiments or operations from one room to another within a school or hospital or for other local uses. Closed circuit TV uses coaxial cables to carry its signals, so it does not require allocation of broadcast frequencies or powerful and expensive transmitting equipment.

Cable TV and Satellites

Commercial programs can also be sent for short distances from a central receiver to individual homes by coaxial cable. The cable contains a larger number of copper tubes, each about three-eighths inch in diameter, with central wires supported by plastic spacers. There are limits to cable television, though. All subscribers need to be connected by wire, which can be quite expensive for outlying homes. Subscribers must pay a monthly fee for the service. And coaxial cables need amplifiers to carry signals more than a few miles.

For the longest distance picture transmission, to carry waves that travel in straight lines around the curves of the earth, large communication satellites operate at frequencies of about 4–6 gigahertz (billion hertz). Communication satellites, first launched in 1964, orbit the earth at an altitude of about 22,000 miles (36,000 km). The current ones (1976) can transmit up to 9,000 telephone calls at a time and can handle up to 12 color-television broadcasts.

It is hoped that in the near future there will be about 50 satellites with hundreds of ground stations. These will provide 100 million voice circuits or 100,000 two-way TV circuits. Then there will be no need for numerous relay stations to amplify and redirect the signals.

Modulation

To send many messages simultaneously along radio wave channels, either up to a satellite and back to earth or from point to point on the ground, several techniques are available. The principal ones are modulation and multiplexing.

Most of us are familiar with the terms AM and FM with relation to radio reception. AM stands for amplitude modulation, FM for frequency modulation. Basically what happens is that low-frequency waves set up by voices or music are used to modulate or adapt the pattern of high-frequency (radio) waves. Either the height (amplitude) or the frequency may be adapted.

Suppose we wish to send a voice message by AM—amplitude modulation. The waves of the voice current (Diagram 1) are added to the radio carrier wave (Diagram 2) in a device called a modulator. This causes the peaks (amplitude) of the radio wave to take on the pattern of the voice waves (Diagram 3). A detector in the radio receiver reverses the modulation process. It recovers the voice signal from the radio carrier wave and passes the pattern of the voice waves along to the loudspeaker, where they emerge as sound waves.

AM broadcasts can be interfered with by competing electrical signals, from lightning to spark plugs in passing automobiles. Fre-

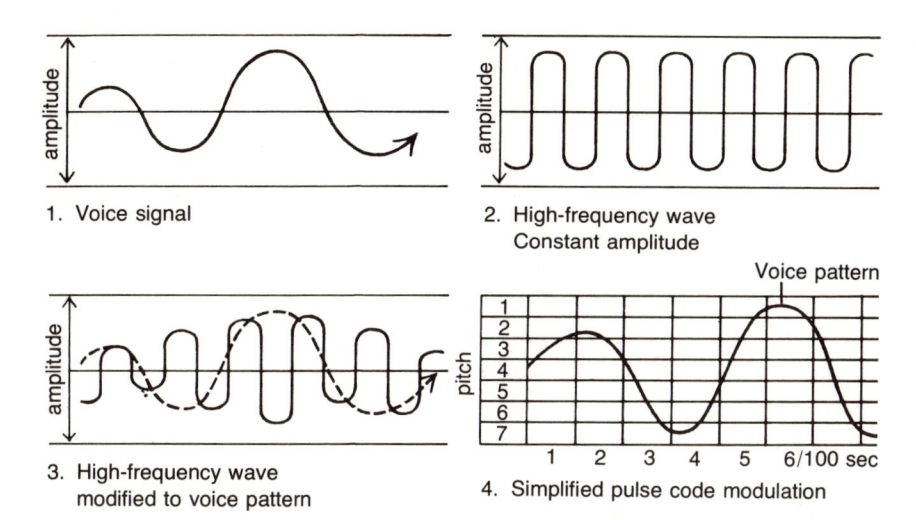

1. Voice signal

2. High-frequency wave
   Constant amplitude

3. High-frequency wave
   modified to voice pattern

4. Simplified pulse code modulation

quency modulation (FM) overcomes much of the noise problem but requires a greater bandwidth. FM changes the frequency of the carrier wave rather than the height, to reflect the pattern of the voice or music.

Pulse code modulation involves sampling the height of the voice or music wave, placing it in one of a range of 127 bands, 8,000 times a second. Each sample rating is translated into a binary number, which consists of a sequence of O's and 1's. These 1 or O electrical pulses are transmitted by the tens of thousands per second and are decoded in the receiver to reproduce the original signal.

A simplified form of pulse code transmission reduces the 127 bands on the wave amplitude scale to a series of seven. The rise and fall of the spoken message is sampled, again thousands of times each second, and the list of band numbers in which the message falls at each sampling is transmitted. At the receiving end these are converted back into the sound ranges they represent. And out comes a sound pattern enough like the original speech to be understandable.

Multiplexing

To see how multiplexing works, let us suppose that we have a circuit with an available bandwidth of 4,000 khz (4 million hertz). A bandwidth this wide will be available only in the range of very short (micro) high-frequency waves. The frequency may be about 6,000 mhz (6 billion cycles per second!). We know that one voice message requires at most 4 khz (4,000 cycles per second) of bandwidth. A 4,000 khz bandwidth can then accommodate 1,000 voice messages side by side. Each voice-channel frequency is "transposed" or stepped up in frequency to fit one of the 1,000 frequency slots that are each 4 khz wide. At the receiving end, each voice channel is transposed in reverse or stepped down in frequency. Then the voice signals are sorted out and distributed to complete 1,000 long-distance telephone connections. That technique is called frequency-division multiplexing.

Time-division multiplexing is newer and more complicated. It involves sampling each channel many times each second. In our example of a large number of voice channels to be carried in a band 4 mhz wide, each channel would be sampled 8,000 times per second, producing one bit of information (to be carried by one cycle) per sample. The 8,000 bits of information times 500 channels would fully occupy the 4 mhz bandwidth available on the microwave carrier. The number of channels is thus reduced, but pulsed signals can tolerate more noise and require less equipment or power. What time-division multiplexing loses in quantity it makes up in quality of the messages.

Codes for Pictures

For decades we have been told that soon our telephones would have pictures as well as sound. The reason personal TV or picture phones have been slow in developing is that sending one TV picture through hones would have pictures as well as sound. The reason personal TV or picture phones have been slow in developing is that sending one TV picture through a series of land microwave stations or a satellite relay station costs about as much as 5,000 long-distance telephone calls.

One possible system for simplifying transmission of changing pictures has been experimentally solved. As described in "Sending Words and Pictures," the TV beam traces a pattern of millions of dots per second on a screen. Engineers working in information or communication theory have decided that a much smaller number of "picture patches" or bits could convey an image that would be sufficient for some purposes.

In everyday life we often can recognize someone we know, at a distance, without being able to see him or her clearly. A limited number of clues as to size, shape and pattern of movement identify the person for us. Similarly, in listening to a conversation we often get the general meaning without hearing every word clearly enough to understand it.

With these observations in mind, engineers have worked out the system of voice transmission described earlier, in which the range of pitches is divided into a few bands. Similarly, pictures are simplified into patterns of small squares. Experiments have been conducted with computers to determine the smallest amount of information that can succeed in making a picture recognizable.

Up to the present (1976) this process has been used more for demonstrations of the principle than for practical purposes. But it seems promising for the future. In the experiments, the picture to be transmitted is divided into squares called picture elements. Each small square is represented as a flat area of some shade of gray. This gray tone is then assigned a binary code signal consisting of a sequence of on-off electrical pulses. Each time that exact gray tone appears in the picture, as the beam scans it, the tone is represented by the same code signal. This is a little like those "paint by the number" patterns in which each area is assigned a number and each number refers to a color to be applied there.

The pattern of signals is transmitted, one row of squares after another, to the receiver—at the speed of light. In the receiver, the pulses are transposed back into gray areas and reassembled. And the result is something basically like the original picture.

The rate at which these picture elements or "bits" can be transmitted is so rapid that the human eye sees the whole reassembled picture arriving simultaneously, as on television. The resulting picture has enough accuracy to satisfy the eye.

Some personal picture phones have been produced, and more could be if people are willing to pay the price. But the price is necessarily high, since each message with even a small picture— with a much smaller number of dots than commercial TV—requires at least 300 voice channels and therefore involves 300 times the expense of an ordinary long-distance call.

A simplified picture transmission process such as the one described above may make picture phones a practical reality in our world tomorrow.

Magnetic Tapes

It is not always necessary to have words and pictures transmitted instantly or "live," as we say of TV programs. Many programs are produced long before we see them on our home TV sets. They are recorded on magnetic tape, which can be mailed to the TV station for broadcasting. This saves expensive long-distance transmission by radio channels.

To record a TV picture and sound on a magnetic tape, the recorder must have a bandwidth of at least 4.5 mhz. It is much like the kind of small sound recorder you may have used. The tape is wider, the movement is faster and it has a different magnetic recording head.

In the television camera, you will recall, light from the scene being photographed "scans" a sensitive screen. Electrons are knocked loose from dot after dot, row upon row, in proportion to the amount of light in each bit of the scene. These electrons are collected as a varying electric current.

To tape the program, this electric current is passed through the coil of wire wound on the magnetic recording head. This produces a magnetic field in the recording head. As the tape is pressed against this head, fine brown particles of iron coating on the tape are magnetized. Each particle is magnetized in an amount corresponding to the strength of the magnetic field (or the electric current from the camera) as it varies.

When the program is to be broadcast from the tape, the tape must be pulled past a magnetic playback head. The magnetized particles of iron set up a varying magnetic field in the playback head, corresponding to the current that went into the recording head. This current can be used to change the number of electrons in a beam that scans the face of the TV picture tube. The chemical coating of the picture tube emits light according to the number of electrons that strike each dot of phosphor. This recreates the pattern of light and dark that entered the lens of the camera—the original scene!

It will soon be possible to buy or rent a tape of any program you would like to see, and play it through your own TV set at home.

Optical Fibers, Lasers and Diodes

Another promising means for transmitting messages for short distances is by means of optical fibers. They will use light waves, which are even higher in frequency than microwaves, for sending messages.

An optical fiber is a fine-spun thread of glass, about the diameter of a human hair. It is transparent and somewhat more dense at the center than at the outside.

Light that is fluctuating like the electric current in a telephone is introduced into an optical fiber from a laser or light-emitting diode. And how do they work? Let us see.

Laser stands for *Light Amplification by Stimulated Emission of Radiation*. High-energy electrons in a gas such as carbon dioxide can cause it to emit light that can be focused in an extremely fine, powerful beam. Powerful laser beams can burn tiny holes in steel plates or cut through a stack of cloth as easily as a scissors can cut thin paper. Other lasers can be used to amplify light waves. Their beams can be modified to carry TV pictures.

Diodes are built from semiconductor crystals very much like those used in transistors. You may have seen them used to display numerals on digital clock faces or electronic calculators. They emit more or less light according to the amount of current that is passed through them. Thus, a TV picture or a multiplexed signal containing a great many telephone conversations can be used to vary the light output from a light-emitting diode or laser. This broadband signal can be transmitted down an optical fiber.

Because optical fibers are so tiny, a great many of them can be assembled into a small bundle and buried underground to carry messages between repeater stations. The problem is that these fibers lose light quickly. At present only about one percent of the original light emerges at the end of a fiber five-eighths of a mile (1 km) long. Small lasers will be available soon that fit onto the end of an optical fiber to act as a repeater-amplifier and to boost the light signal on its way.

When these small lasers are generally available, it seems certain that these very compact optical systems will be carrying millions of voice conversations and hundreds or thousands of TV messages for short distances within cities.

LET THE COMPUTER DO IT

It is morning in the home of tomorrow. Before the two children of the family leave for school and the mother and father leave for work, the household must be set in order. This is a simple matter. Someone—perhaps, but not necessarily, the mother—sits down at the kitchen area computer for the main tasks. Of course putting away clothes and similar duties must be taken care of by each person individually.

One list of chores and another list of food and household needs are tacked on a bulletin board close to the computer. A flick of the switch turns on the instrument. Whoever is operating it taps out the grocery list in code. The list is transmitted to the neighborhood market by the computer. The items are automatically assembled there, to be delivered in the afternoon.

Instructions for turning on and off the vacuum air freshener and duster, the dishwasher and other household equipment are tapped out on another keyboard.

Business tasks such as paying bills, balancing the family checking account and other mathematical problems are taken care of by tapping out numbers on a "touch-tone" telephone, which puts the caller in contact with a central computer in a nearby bank.

Mother or father may in fact be working at home, using equipment of this sort. Employees can work in the peace and quiet of their homes on certain projects, instead of commuting to a central office. They can confer with other workers by conference telephone with picture attachment. Figures or other information they transmit by touch telephone, tapping out a code as simply as today an airline reservation clerk can tap out information about the flight you want. Within seconds a reply can be received from a central computer.

Pre-Computer Equipment

The computer is the home of tomorrow. Even today, systems are already available for transmitting information from a computer or other automatic device by telephone. But they are still—in the mid-1970s—not very practical for home use.

Use of a central computer by families at home who tap out information on their touch telephones, for example, has been tried. But the touch telephones are by no means universally in use, and communicating by tapping out one letter or number at a time is quite slow.

Another pre-computer communicator is the teletypewriter. It has been widely used for many years among subscribing offices. But it uses equipment that is bulky and noisy and quite expensive. The teletype operator types out a message in the ordinary characters and spaces of a usual typewriter. The teletypewriter encodes these typed characters as groups of electrical "on-or-off" pulses. Each of these "on-or-off" or "yes-or-no" choices is the equivalent of a binary digit or "bit."

The teletypewriter transmits and receives bits at the typist's speed—up to 120 words per minute. Some other types of equipment are more rapid. They store information by typing out in advance many of these bits. Once the equipment is turned on for transmittal, it sends messages faster than fingers can type. At the other end of the circuit another machine translates the electrical impulses back into letters and spaces. It types them out again for humans to read.

The teletypewriter or its swifter variations are very useful between many branch offices of large companies. But the equipment is too bulky and expensive for home use at this time.

Tape to Phone

An ordinary telephone can be used to transmit information directly from a computer's magnetic tape. But a piece of additional

A first step in the move to revolutionize book production: A typist at a desk-top unit can now prepare copy for printing in any of 125 type sizes and styles. (Photo courtesy of IBM)

equipment called a digital sub set is needed. A computer, as you know, must be given instructions in the form of holes in a card or tape or by means of magnetic tape. At each point on a punch card or tape either there is a hole or there is none. A digital sub set can convert this pattern of punched holes into tones. The code of electrical pulses—or tones—can be transmitted more rapidly than the taped bits on an electrical teletypewriter.

Another method is already in operation for sending computerized information by telephone. Before putting in your telephone call you feed your information onto a magnetic tape recorder. Then you put through a regular long-distance call. When the other party is ready to receive, you turn on your tape recorder.

Sometimes the message can be transmitted backward, so that it is ready to play when it is wound onto a tape recorder at the receiving end. This saves rewinding. This method can be used for a voice recording that is picked up by a tape machine at the other end of the line. It can also be used with information in the form of magnetized spots on computer tape, then converted to tones and back again to spots on tape.

There are plenty of methods available for communicating information efficiently. It will be possible for many businesses to operate their offices and keep records largely through communication between machines. This will make possible welcome savings in paper and filing space.

"The problem is the expense of the terminals," a communications engineer explains. "The cost of receiving and transmitting equipment is holding back the spread of many data services. For example, a secretary, in order to type in form to be transmitted by machine, needs a typewriter that costs about $3,000. A price of $300 to $500 could make the system widely useful in homes as well as small offices.

"We are due for a revolutionary advance in the means for recording information in form a machine can read," the engineer continues. "This is going to be a very exciting field for young people who are in school today."

Phone a Document

It should be possible to send a whole document or a picture by telephone as a unit. In fact, the technology for picture phones is available. It is now used on a limited basis in cable television. There pictures go from a central source (ctv) to subscribers x, y and z. But home or office communication with pictures between individual subscribers x, y and z is not yet practical. The main bottleneck, as has been noted, is the cost.

Optical fibers promise to improve transmission soon. At present, though, the expensive cathode ray tubes are still needed. Printing mechanisms to receive the picture and transpose it into usable form are bulky and noisy as well as costly. More work is needed on all this equipment to improve its usability for mass production.

Also needed is a system that will transmit pictures stored on microfilm. Microfiche, which is microfilm in sheets the size of a filing card, is available. A (4- × 6-inch) card of this material can hold 60 pages of text or pictures. Libraries already have tabletop devices that can enlarge a single page at a time for individual readers. And books on microfiche can be shown to groups in schools, with each page enlarged for easy viewing. But for use with these viewers, the microfilm holding the pictures in miniature must be on hand. A

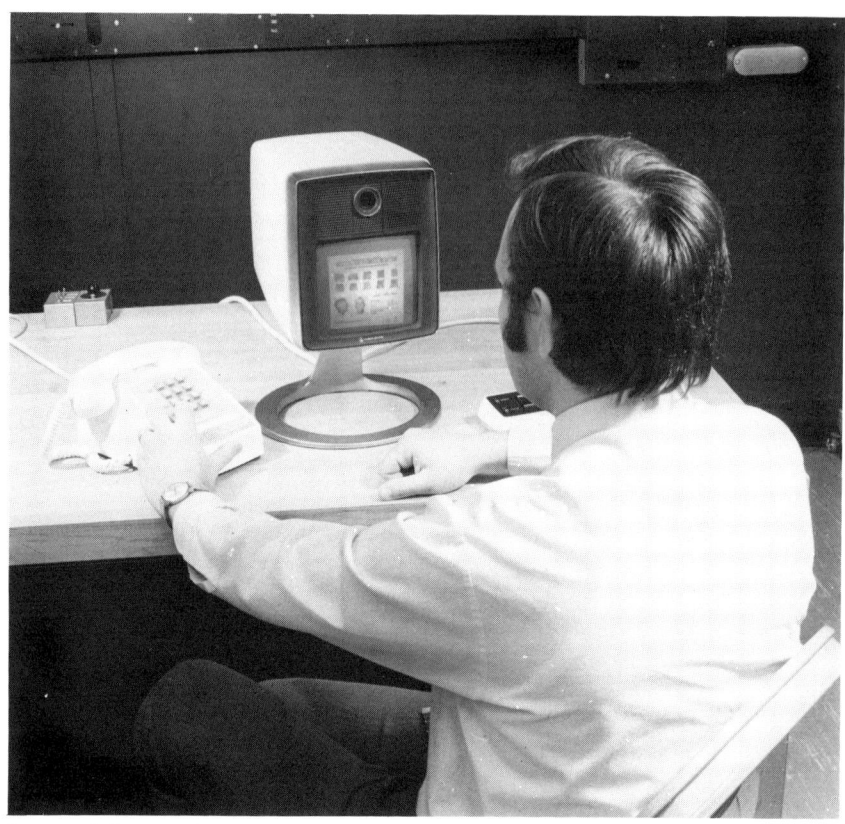

Images of objects such as microfilm, bank checks, electrocardiograms and engineering drawings can be viewed on picturephone sets. (Photo courtesy of Bell Labs)

whole new world will open up in the use of microfiche once its small pictures can be transmitted easily, clearly and instantly across long distances.

By 1973 some government agencies had microfiche cards that held 96 pages of printed material but with some blurring of detail. In terms of the future usefulness of microfiche, the number of pages per card is not as important as the long-distance transmission. When single pages can be transmitted instantly across the miles from one office or school or library to another, it will mean a tremendous saving in burdensome files, stacks and shelves of paper. And it will greatly lighten the burden of postal services. This process will also revolutionize a good deal of book production.

Tomorrow's Books

The writer switches off the typewriter, draws a deep breath and stretches his (or her) weary shoulders. He has just finished typing the final draft of a manuscript. He has typed this last draft on a special machine, more expensive than a regular typewriter. At his side is the finished manuscript. But it is not in the form of a neat stack of typing paper. Instead, it is a file box full of magnetic cards. (Another similar machine might use tape instead.) The manuscript has been transformed by the typing machine from words into binary code that can be read by a computer.

Microfiche cards are organized by a grid system, with horizontal rows labeled by letter and vertical columns labeled by number. (Photo courtesy of University of Chicago Press Text/Fiche Publication)

The writer contacts his publisher by long-distance telephone. In the publisher's plant, the tapes are fed into the publisher's editing and proofing equipment, at a rate of 1,200 characters per second. The edited copy is then transmitted to a computer that sets the copy in type, turning it back into words again and producing finished pages. These in turn can be stored compactly on microfiche cards, to be reproduced in any desired quantity.

Before many years have passed it seems likely that every home will have a viewer with which these microfiche cards can be read. They will no longer be limited to schools and libraries. Many of our magazines, pamphlets and books will come in the form of small packs of cards. They will be very easy to store or to dispose after reading. And incidentally, they will save many trees that would otherwise have been cut to supply paper mills.

Computer Uses

The uses for computers are numberless. In school a teaching machine can guide a student in learning to solve problems. It can respond so sensitively to the student's attempts, step by step, that it can be more helpful and stimulating on a one-to-one basis than a busy, distracted teacher can be.

In an engineering office a computer can speed through laborious calculations almost instantly. It can swiftly try out all sorts of design possibilities in the planning of new buildings, airplanes, highways or transportation systems.

In a library or office, as we have seen, tapes or cards can store vast quantitites of information compactly and efficiently. And the computer can swiftly and precisely sort out the facts that fill a specific need.

In a clinic a computer given medical information about a patient can produce a correct diagnosis.

From your own experience you can probably add other uses to this brief list. The speed of development of new uses for the computer of tomorrow and the wide spread of present ones depends on price and value factors more than technology.

Quite a lot of work has been done in an effort to "teach" computers to accept instructions spoken into a telephone. But progress is slow and discouraging. Part of the trouble is that English is a very complex language. No one has been able to program a computer to understand a voice message. After all, your brain is much more complex and capable than any computer ever built. And don't you sometimes have difficulty understanding directions or instructions someone gives you in English?

"A computer," says an engineer, "is terribly stupid. It has no judgment. You must tell it in complete and exact detail what it is to do for you or it may work for hours at a meaningless task."

To most of us it seems remarkable enough that a machine can respond correctly to coded instructions in an "on-off" alphabet, that when an instruction says "add" or "divide" it can do so accurately and with incredible speed. Most of us will not feel a strong need to speak directly to a computer in plain English and have it respond.

Still, there are reasons for concern about computers. One criticism is that computers are dehumanizing life. Automation of industry means fewer jobs, especially for those with limited skills. It also means that any one worker is involved with such a small segment of the production process that there is no pride in the finished product. As a result workers are bored and feel little responsibility for doing their best.

Some people fear that automating shopping, business, health care and education will eliminate too many of our day-to-day contacts with other human beings. They think we will all end up sitting alone, feeding machines to talk to other machines.

Planners reply that what is being eliminated is principally the monotonous drudgery of life. If a wage-earner does not have to spend two hours a day commuting to and from work on crowded streets or highways, there will be more time for recreation with family and friends. If fewer workers are required on assembly lines to tighten bolts and turn screws, new occupations will offer opportunities for them to work in more creative ways. Gardening, woodworking, painting and other handcrafts will attract more people. They will have more opportunities to communicate feelings and emotions, to share their hopes and their pleasure in beauty. Music, dance and all the arts are ways of communicating in human terms that no computer can match.

Perhaps technology may free people, in our world tomorrow, to deal on a personal basis with some of the very human problems that are often brushed aside in today's tension-filled world.

AFTERWORD

"The necessary technology is available," we are told, in relation to situation after situation, as we consider prospects for life in tomorrow's world. Few, if any, new inventions are needed for development of mass-transportation systems, energy-saving business buildings and new ways of sharing information. The things that need attention and change are our patterns of living together. Persuading people to change their ways of living is more difficult than developing a new scientific process.

The heart of the problem is that while human beings have been on earth for about 40,000 years, during most of those years there were only scatterings of people wandering about in small family groups, hunting food. It was about 8,000 years ago that people learned to cultivate food and began to live in small settlements. But it was only about 200 years ago that the scientific and industrial revolution began to pull people together into larger and larger communities. At the same time the average life-span was lengthened and the world's population increased.

People simply have not adapted their ways of living to these new social realities. For example, many people still feel that it is their right—even their duty—to have big families. Actually there is hardly enough food and certainly not enough good housing for the billions of people who exist today. To continue to let world population grow unchecked can lead only to famine and great distress.

Constant crowding is one particularly difficult condition for human beings. Now and then we like to gather together in crowds, but just as often we like to be able to be quietly by ourselves. We cannot live constantly in crowded conditions and remain healthy and happy any more than other animals can.

An example of what overcrowding can do is found in the report of an experiment with a community of mice that was conducted by United States government psychologists. The mice were supplied with plenty of food and water. They were protected from enemies, disease and the weather. For a while everything seemed ideal. Protected from all dangers, their population increased rapidly— doubling and redoubling much as the worldwide human population is doing today.

Before long there were so many mice that, in the words of the psychologists, "there were no social roles for the young to fill." Female mice, their nests overcrowded with young, became quarrelsome and domineering. They pushed their babies out of the nest instead of giving them tender care. Males became lazy, unresponsive hermits.

Family life broke down, and the mice lost interest even in producing young. Once the males gave up their leadership, the mice seemed to drift apart. The nests and the cages were no longer kept clean. At last the whole colony simply died.

Human beings are not mice. It is dangerous to carry the parallel too far. But there are two lessons people can learn from this experiment. The first is that there can be no long-range happiness ahead unless population growth is controlled.

The other lesson is that every human being needs a social role. To be a fully developed person one must have a place in some community. One must be able to communicate thoughts and feelings to others and to receive their ideas in return.

Providing every person with an opportunity to be a productive member of a community is more important than providing material possessions, entertainment and plenty of holidays.

The sense of belonging somewhere as an individual defines our existence. Modern equipment and technology can broaden our lives, but they cannot take the place of human warmth. The secret of success for humankind lies in our learning to live together. That is the challenge—and the hope—for tomorrow's world.

SELECTED READING LIST

Blair, Thomas L., *The International Urban Crisis*. New York: Hill & Wang, 1974

Chinoy, E., ed., *The Urban Future*. New York: Lieber-Atherton, 1973

Glaab, C. M., and Brown, A. T., *A History of Urban America*. New York: Collier-Macmillan, 1967

Hellman, Harold, *Communications in the World of the Future*. New York: M. Evans, 1969

———, *Energy in the World of the Future*. New York: M. Evans, 1973

———, *Transportation in the World of the Future*. New York: M. Evans, 1968

Hinrichs, Noel, ed., *Population, Environment and People*. New York: McGraw-Hill, 1971

Jacobs, Jane, *The Death and Life of Great American Cities*. New York: Random House, 1961

Kone, Eugene, and Jordan, Helene, eds., *The Greatest Adventure: Basic Research That Shapes Our Lives*. New York: Rockefeller University Press, 1974

Liston, Robert A., *Downtown: Our Challenging Urban Problems*. New York: Delacorte, 1965

Luna, Charles, *The UTU Handbook of Transportation in America*. New York: Popular Library, 1971

Maddox, Brenda, *Beyond Babel: New Directions in Communications*. New York: Simon and Schuster, 1972

Maddox, John, *The Doomsday Syndrome*. New York: McGraw-Hill, 1972

Meadows, Donella; Meadows, Dennis; Randers, Jorgen; and Behrens, William, *The Limits to Growth: A Report for the Club of Rome's Project on the Predicament of Mankind*. New York: Universe Books, 1972

Reich, Charles A., *The Greening of America*. New York: Random House, 1970

Ridley, A., *Living in Cities*. New York: John Day, 1972

Safdie, Moshe, *Beyond Habitat*. Cambridge, Mass: The MIT Press, 1970

Spencer, Cornelia, *Keeping Ahead of Machines: The Human Side of the Automation Revolution*. New York: John Day, 1965

Stone, Tabor R., *Beyond the Automobile: Reshaping the Transportation Environment*. Englewood Cliffs, N.J.: Prentice-Hall, 1971

Theobald, Robert, *Habit and Habitat: A Call for Fundamental Changes to Solve the Environmental Crisis*. Englewood Cliffs, N.J.: Prentice-Hall, 1972

Toffler, Alvin, *Future Shock*. New York: Random House, 1970

Ward, Barbara, and Dubos, Rene, *Only One Earth; The Care and Maintenance of a Small Planet*. New York: W. W. Norton, 1972

INDEX

157